Cooperative Group Problem Solving

by Douglass Campbell

illustrated by Bill Singleton

FS-10134 Cooperative Group Problem Solving

23740 Hawthorne Blvd.
Torrance, CA 90505

Table of Contents

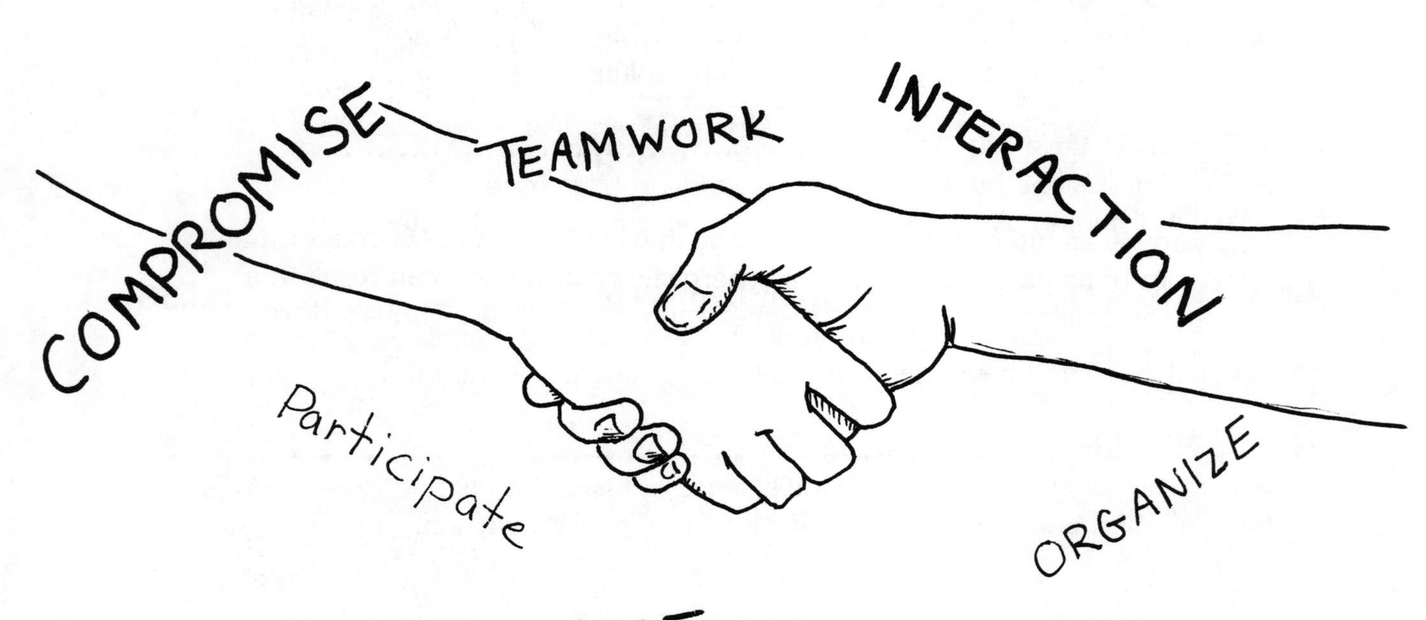
COMPROMISE
TEAMWORK
INTERACTION
Participate
ORGANIZE
COOPERATE

To the Teacher

Every teacher is in awe of the potential of the human being to grow and learn. To move from a dependent child to an independent adult is a process in which good teachers play an important role. Among the many tools, skills, and attitudes that are helpful in the transformation process are what we might call "the problem-solving skills." Instead of continually depending upon others for solutions, the students generate their own. Hopefully, we can help prepare them for this independent and enthusiastic outlook.

Part of this successful transformation includes interacting with other individuals. A powerful source of energy comes when groups of individuals can "share their experiences and talents" and focus them in a problem-solving mode. In addition to the "problem at hand," many other lessons are learned. Learning how to listen, how to assume different roles, how to cooperate, and how to get things done are just some of the benefits resulting from team problem-solving efforts.

Synergy is an interesting form of energy in which the whole is greater than the sum of its parts. Simply put, a synergistic environment can result in a group of ordinary people producing extraordinary results. Thousands of great teachers have learned that some of the most significant learning comes in situations where students collectively solved problems, invented things, and produced their own learning environment.

Cooperative Group Problem Solving is intended to be exactly what the title suggests–a series of instructional techniques for understanding group dynamics and bringing them to bear as a problem-solving unit. High interest projects are used to apply the learning gained from the various techniques introduced.

The early units are intended to illustrate how failure is often the result of poor team dynamics. In addition, they illustrate how group problem-solving results are often better than those of individuals. Students are given interesting "life or death" problems and can compare the solutions of individuals and those of teams.

"Pulling the Strings" is a fascinating activity which clearly illustrates the necessary dynamics for a successful team and what happens if any of those dynamics are missing.

In school athletics, many team members must play several roles. The team quarterback may also play in the defensive backfield. The pitcher may also be the shortstop for some games. Some of the activities will illustrate how team problem solving will also require people who can play different roles. Sometimes a team needs certain talents. Everyone cannot be the team leader all of the time, nor can everyone be the person who completed the project.

One of the more interesting projects suggests that a barrier to learning and effective group interaction stems from spending your time thinking of what you will say when it is your turn to speak instead of listening to what others have to contribute.

Problem definition, fact-finding, solution testing, and strategic thinking are all tools introduced in activities. Each of these skills is applied in some "high interest" activity which is more likely to generate enthusiasm while learning. You may wish to read aloud the discussion questions which follow each activity. Students will learn a great deal about their group problem-solving skills as they discuss their answers. As is always the case with great teachers, you may wish to modify the activities into ones which you sense are more interesting or relevant. Feel free to do so.

The "Bingo" activity is one which could produce many valuable teaching aids intended to result in learning victories throughout the school year. Hopefully, it will result in a string of success stories which encourage more of the same.

Quite simply put, people are more likely to "buy into" something to which they have contributed. Getting into the habit of contributing to their own growth, learning, and development may lead students to a more responsible attitude toward themselves and their lives.

I envy the enjoyment that you have in the learning enterprise where it is likely that great things can be developed in a partnership between students and great teachers.

THE GREAT FLOOR OF DIMINIMUS ISLAND

Objectives

- To illustrate the effect of poor group organization.
- To illustrate a situation where the combined knowledge of the team can solve a problem but where, through poor team organization, the problem is often difficult to solve.

Procedure

Divide the class into several groups. Groups can range in size from six to eight per group. Each class member is given the general description of Diminimus Island, a strange land dating back three thousand years and only recently discovered.

Once the descriptions are read, information cards are dealt out in each group in the same manner as dealing a deck of cards. Each card represents a piece of information about this land that has been learned by archeologists. Each team member should have four or five cards. NOTE: There should be as many sets of cards as there are groups. **It should be emphasized that individuals read their cards but not show them to anyone else. They can share their information orally with other members of their group.**

The team is given 30 minutes to determine the name of the god or goddess for whom the temple was constructed in the year 1007 B.C.

What to Expect

Typically, chaos takes place unless someone in a group takes charge and starts some form of organization. As the 30 minutes are almost up, students will ask you for clarification. Some might simply quit. In some groups, everyone will be talking at once. Spend time in each group without commenting. If asked, simply reaffirm the instructions.

Materials Required

Make as many copies of the information pages as there are groups if you divide your class by six. Cut each of the information pages into individual, numbered cards. Keep each group of cards separate from the other.

Approximate Time

The introduction to the activity should take approximately 5 minutes. The group meeting should last exactly 30 minutes. The follow-up can last as long as meaningful questions and dialogue continue.

Discussion Questions

1. **Which group has an answer to the question and can prove it?**
   Chances are that no group had time to determine the answer. If this is the case, continue with these questions. Later, the answer is outlined.

2. **How would you evaluate your group's performance in arriving at the answer?**
   Hopefully, some students recognize that their group did not seem to be organized enough to sort out the information to arrive at an answer.

3. **What did you think you were supposed to do in the group?**
   Students realize that they were to determine an answer to the question. It will be a good sign if students recognize that a complete lack of organization prevented them from sorting out the information. It would have been helpful if someone had been named leader. Some groups may have appointed one or a leader may have emerged, but probably not in time to determine the answer.

4. **What could have been done so that each group could have solved the problem?**
   See if students can recognize that they needed some organization. It would have been helpful to have a leader or chairperson who might have kept the group focused on the problem. It would have been helpful to have some working procedures or system with which to proceed toward a solution.

The following is an outline of the necessary questions to address. Have students provide the information as it is required.

A. **What has to be determined?**
We have to know the day of the week on which the temple floor was completed so that we will know the name of the god or goddess for whom the temple was constructed.

B. **How should we proceed?**
We must know the size of the floor and how long it takes a crew to construct it. We know that the temple was named for the god or goddess who corresponded to the day on which the floor was completed.

C. **Who has information on the size of the floor?**
The size of the floor is 20 derbles x 10 derbles. Since a derble is equal to 10 feet, the floor is 100 x 200 feet or 20,000 square feet in area.

D. **How many people were involved in building the floor?**
One work squad was assigned to the floor. Although there are six workers in a crew, one of them does not set block.

E. **How long did it take to construct the floor?**
One worker can set 40 blocks in a nurn. There are 10 working nurns in a day. Given 20 loinks of rest period, this leaves 8 working nurns in a day since 10 loinks equal 1 nurn. Therefore, a worker can set 40 x 8 or 320 blocks in a day. A crew of 5 can set 1,600 blocks in a day. Since a block is 1 square foot in area, there were 20,000 blocks in the floor. With this, we know that it took 12 1/2 days to set the floor (20,000 ÷ 1,600).

F. **What day of the week was the work completed?**
We know that there are five days in a week, but there is no work done on day five. We know that work on the wall started on the first day of the week. Therefore, work was completed on the FIRST day of the FOURTH week. Since this is Adas, the temple was built in honor of Adas, the god of trees.

INFORMATION PAGE: CUT ALONG DOTTED LINES

1. The basic measurement of time on Diminimus Island is a day.

2. On Diminimus Island, a day is divided into nurns and loinks.

3. The floor in the Great Hall is 20 derbles long.

4. A derble is equal to 10 feet.

5. The floor is 10 derbles wide.

6. The temple was named in honor of the god (goddess) associated with the day on which the floor in the Great Hall was completed.

7. The floor is constructed of stone blocks.

8. Each block is one foot square.

9. The first day of the week is called "Adas," named in honor of Adas, the god of the trees.

10. The second day of the week is called "Edas." It is named after Edas, the goddess of bushes and berries.

11. The third day of the week is called "Idos." Idos is the powerful god who created the aardvark.

12. The fourth day of the week is called "Odos." It is named after the warrior goddess Odos, who invented the rolling stone.

13. Day five on Diminimus Island is called "Udos." Ud and Os were the twin gods of bowling, a game invented on Diminimus Island.

14. There are five days in a week.

15. A working day on Diminimus Island is 10 nurns.

16. Each worker takes rest periods during the work day totalling 20 loinks.

17. There are10 loinks in a nurn.

18. An individual in a labor squad can set 40 blocks per nurn.

19. There was only one work squad assigned to setting the floor.

20. Each work squad has six members of skilled stonesetters.

21. Each work squad has a priest who does not work but who attends to religious duties.

22. No work is performed on Udos.

23. What do the workers wear when they work?

24. The workers always wear a nerf over a matching koob.

25. Do workers ever get a day off or a vacation?

26. Workers get vacations only when temples are completed.

27. Green is a color with special religious significance.

28. There are an equal number of kabofoos in a work group.

THE GREAT FLOOR OF DIMINIMUS ISLAND

Signs of an advanced civilization have been discovered on an obscure island in the Indian Ocean. Archeologists from around the world have descended on Diminimus Island to investigate the temple that was discovered. Because of the local government's policies of limited foreign visitation rights, information about the temple is sketchy.

We do know that all that remains intact of the temple is the floor in the great hall. It is composed of solid stone. The stone was perfectly cut and placed without anything to bind it together. Except for the wear of centuries of exposure, the floor is still completely intact.

Most ancient temples were built to honor important gods or goddesses. Knowing which gods are honored with temples tells us what was important to the people. For example, a warlike people would probably have a temple honoring its god of war. One of the mysteries about this find is the deity to whom the temple is dedicated. It will be the responsibility of your team to determine this information.

To acquaint you with this archeological discovery, you will be given information related to the people of Diminimus Island. You may discuss this information with others in your group but do not show them your information cards.

You will have 30 minutes for your team to determine the answer to this question: For which deity was the temple of Diminimus Island constructed? Before you begin, read your information cards and then put them away.

LOST ON THE SIXTH MOON OF THE JUSTINIAN SYSTEM

Objectives

- To demonstrate that problem solving is often more effective when approached by a group than by an individual. With certain types of problems, the collective experience and knowledge of the group is an advantage.
- To begin setting the groundwork for effective team dynamics.

Procedure

Distribute the first page titled "Lost on the Sixth Moon of the Justinian System." Each student should read the material and order a list of 15 pieces of equipment according to the importance of each for survival. When this is complete, students should be arranged into three or four teams. It shall be the responsibility of each team to arrive at a consensus ranking of the same items. Individuals in the group can explain the reasons for their rankings and persuade others to change their rankings. Distribute the second page titled "Tally Sheet." Have students copy their ranking from their first page onto the first column of their Tally Sheet. Assign one member of each team to record the team ranking. When each team has finished, make sure that all individuals record the team ranking in the second column of their Tally Sheet.

Distribute the third and fourth pages titled "Survival Ranking" and "The Results." Working as individuals again, students can record the expert ranking in the third column. They can review the reasons for the choices made by NASA experts.

To determine whether the individual or group rankings provided the highest probability for survival, students can calculate their Disaster Points by writing the difference between their ranking and the expert ranking in the fourth column. For example, if a student ranked the cigarette lighter a 2 and the expert ranking is 15, the Disaster Points are 13, the difference between the two. Complete this for all 15 items and then total the column. This becomes the individual score. Individuals can repeat this procedure comparing the team rankings with the experts. A completed Tally Sheet might appear as follows:

	You	Team	Expert	You/Expert	Team/Expert
A cigarette lighter	5	12	15	10	3
Concentrated food	7	2	4	3	2
60 feet of nylon rope	9	7	6	3	1
Signal flares	11	6	10	1	4
A magnetic compass	2	11	14	12	3
Six 50-pound tanks of oxygen	1	1	1	0	0
A case of dehydrated milk	12	12	12	0	0
Parachute silk	13	13	8	5	5
A solar-powered heating unit	3	14	13	10	1
A 357 magnum pistol	6	8	11	5	3
A map of this moon	8	5	3	5	2
A self-inflating life raft	15	10	9	6	1
Five gallons of water	10	3	2	8	1
First aid kit	14	9	7	7	2
Solar-powered FM two-way radio	4	4	5	1	1
Total				76	29

Once completed, check individual scores on the "Results" page to determine each student's fate. "Xs" can also be entered on the appropriate line to determine their team fate.

What to Expect

Some students might be embarrassed in their team meeting when they learn that some of their responses did not take into account conditions found on the moon. Because of this, many may want to change their individual responses. It is important to clarify that CHANGES CANNOT BE MADE IN INDIVIDUAL RANKINGS ONCE THE GROUP MEETING BEGINS.

You may have to assist groups in coming to a consensus. If a group has difficulty, it can simply vote for its choice. Explain that students are to vote for the most logical choice, not the person giving the choice.

You will probably find that the team score is lower than the individual scores. The lower the score, the greater the chances for survival. (See Disaster Scale in Discussion Questions.)

Most problems will come from a confusion over the scoring. You can give examples, shown earlier, on the chalkboard.

Materials Required	Only individual copies of the student materials are required.
Approximate Time	The entire activity can range in time from 40 to 60 minutes.

Discussion Questions

1. **How many individuals had scores higher than that of their team?**

   Most groups will find that the majority of individuals had scores higher than that of the group. The point of this exercise is to illustrate that the team score is usually (not always) lower (better) than most individual scores.

2. **What expert rankings surprised you? (You did not realize that the item was that important or unimportant.)**

   Many forget that there is no oxygen on the moon. Also, the lack of a magnetic field and problems associated with weightlessness are often overlooked.

3. **Read your score aloud along with the consequences and compare that with your team's score.**

   Students should volunteer to read their individual scores (DISASTER POINTS) along with the consequences and then give their team's score.

4. **What good decisions did your group make that you did not?**
   Let students frankly admit that some of the team responses were more appropriate than theirs.

5. **What is your reaction to this exercise?**

   It may be that some teams did not work effectively. What were the reasons for this? If a team worked effectively, how did the members achieve this effectiveness?

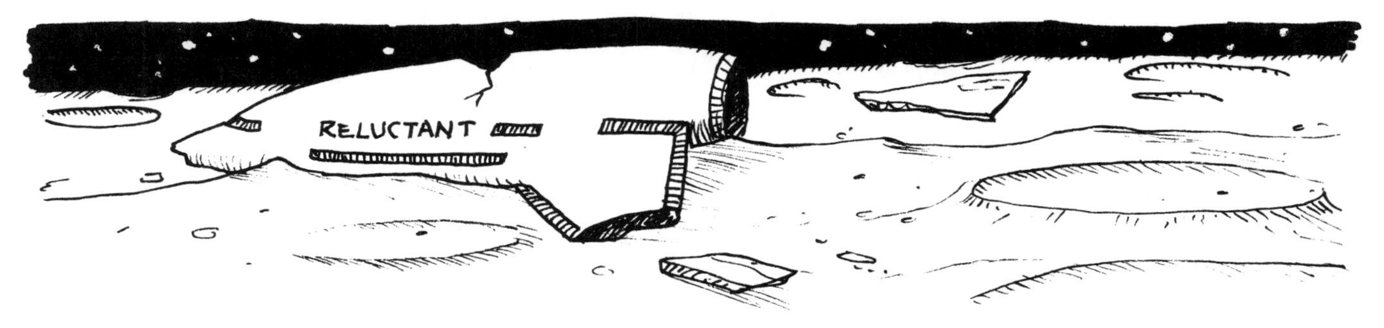

Name________________________________

LOST ON THE SIXTH MOON OF THE JUSTINIAN SYSTEM

You are a crew member of the spaceship *Reluctant.* Your mission has been to search for life forms in space and to return safely to Earth. This mission has been jeopardized because of problems with cooling systems in your spaceship. You have been forced to land 175 miles from your space station, which is on the lighted surface of this moon. Because of a difficult landing, your crew has been forced to evacuate quickly. Moments after the evacuation, an explosion destroyed most of the contents of your spaceship. All that remain are the 15 items listed below.

Your crew's survival depends on reaching the space station. You must choose the most important items from the surviving gear, those which will have the most value in reaching the space station.

Place a number 1 alongside the most important item, number 2 by the second most important, and so on through number 15, the least important.

_____A cigarette lighter
_____Concentrated food
_____60 feet of nylon rope
_____Signal flares
_____A magnetic compass
_____Six 50-pound tanks of oxygen
_____A case of canned milk
_____Parachute silk
_____A solar-powered heating unit
_____A 357 magnum pistol
_____A map of this moon
_____A self-inflating life raft
_____5 gallons of water
_____First-aid kit
_____Solar-powered FM two-way radio

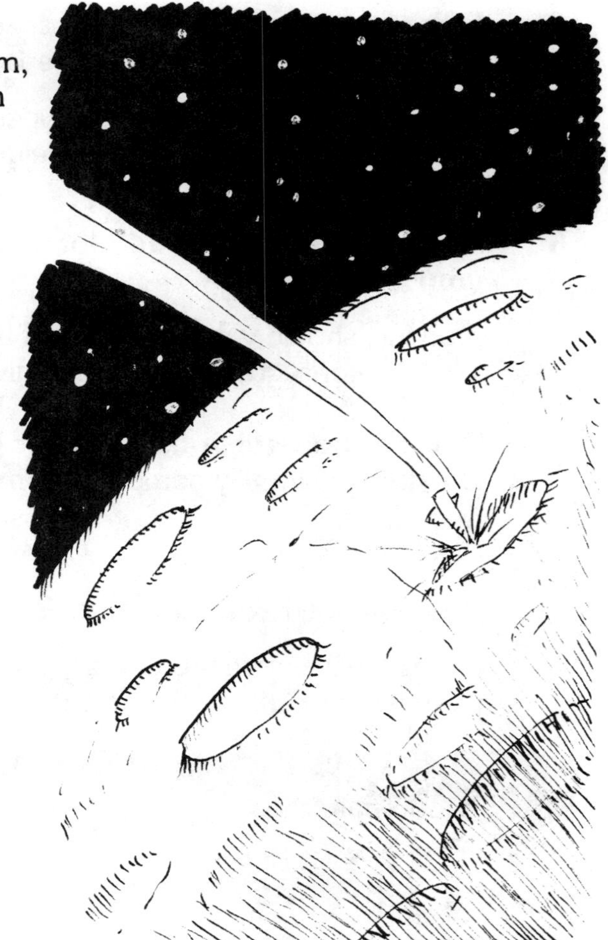

Name________________________________

TALLY SHEET

Instructions: Each group shall meet and discuss their rankings. It shall be the responsibility of each team to arrive at a "team" response. This can be done by discussing each item and voting for the most appropriate choice. Some individuals may wish to justify their choices prior to each vote. Enter the team choice in the Team column.

	You	Team	Expert	You/Expert	Team/Expert
A cigarette lighter	___	___	___	___	___
Concentrated food	___	___	___	___	___
60 feet of nylon rope	___	___	___	___	___
Signal flares	___	___	___	___	___
A magnetic compass	___	___	___	___	___
Six 50-pound tanks of oxygen	___	___	___	___	___
A case of dehydrated milk	___	___	___	___	___
Parachute silk	___	___	___	___	___
A solar-powered heating unit	___	___	___	___	___
A 357 magnum pistol	___	___	___	___	___
A map of this moon	___	___	___	___	___
A self-inflating life raft	___	___	___	___	___
5 gallons of water	___	___	___	___	___
First-aid kit	___	___	___	___	___
Solar-powered FM two-way radio	___	___	___	___	___
TOTAL				___	___

DISASTER POINTS:

Disaster points are the differences in your (team) score and the expert's. To calculate your chances of survival

A. Enter the expert's score shown on the next handout. Review the expert explanations.

B. Compare the numerical difference between your ranking and the expert's ranking for each item.

C. Write the difference in the You/Expert column on the appropriate line. (For example, if you ranked something a 5 and the expert rated it a 9, you have 4 disaster points.)

D. Total the last two columns. This represents your total disaster score and that of your team.

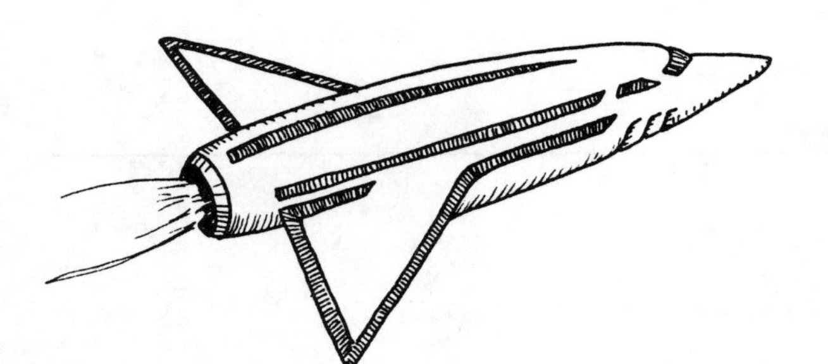

Name ____________________________

SURVIVAL RANKING

The following are the choices of NASA experts on the importance of the remaining items. This ranking represents the best choice for survival of the team. Included with the selections are the reasons for the choices. Enter this ranking in the expert column of your tally sheet.

ITEM	REASONING	NASA RANK
A cigarette lighter	No oxygen on moon to sustain a flame.	**15**
Concentrated food	Excellent for supplying the energy needs of the team.	**4**
60 feet of nylon rope	Useful in scaling cliffs and tying injured people together.	**6**
Signal flares	Useful if you get within sight of the space station.	**10**
A magnetic compass	The magnetic field on moon is not polarized; therefore, the compass is worthless.	**14**
Six 50-pound tanks of oxygen	This is the most important requirement to sustain the life of your team.	**1**
A case of canned milk	Just a bulky duplication of food concentrates.	**12**
Parachute silk	Protection from the elements.	**8**
A solar-powered heating unit	Not useful on the dark side of the moon.	**13**
A 357 magnum pistol	Possibly useful for propulsion.	**11**
A map of this moon	The primary means of navigation.	**3**
A self-inflating life raft	The carbon dioxide bottle in the life raft may be useful for propulsion.	**9**
Five gallons of water	Necessary for great liquid loss when you reach the lighted side of the moon.	**2**
First-Aid kit	Helpful in case of injury and to assist those who were injured.	**7**
Solar-powered FM two-way radio	Useful only with line of sight communication.	**5**

Name ____________________________

THE RESULTS

On the appropriate line below, place a checkmark which corresponds to your score and an "X" for your team score. Read the consequences of your individual choices and compare them with your team's consequences.

	Score	Consequences
____	0-25	Your entire team was returned safely to the space station. You were declared a hero for such outstanding leadership.
____	26-31	Your entire team was returned safely although two members had to be treated for exhaustion and minor injuries.
____	32-37	You will be hospitalized for several months. You will be happy to know that the other members of your team will leave the hospital before you.
____	38-43	At your funeral the other members of the team spoke highly of your achievements. In the years to come, they may resume normal activities.
____	44-49	Only one returned. When she recovers, your fate may be known. There is some discussion of sending a search party to return your remains.
____	50-60	The entire nation observed a moment of silence in memory of your brave efforts and that of your team. You will never be forgotten.
____	61+	NASA has determined that this type of space exploration should be discontinued until they can find a higher quality astronaut.

BASKETBALL IN THE SNOW

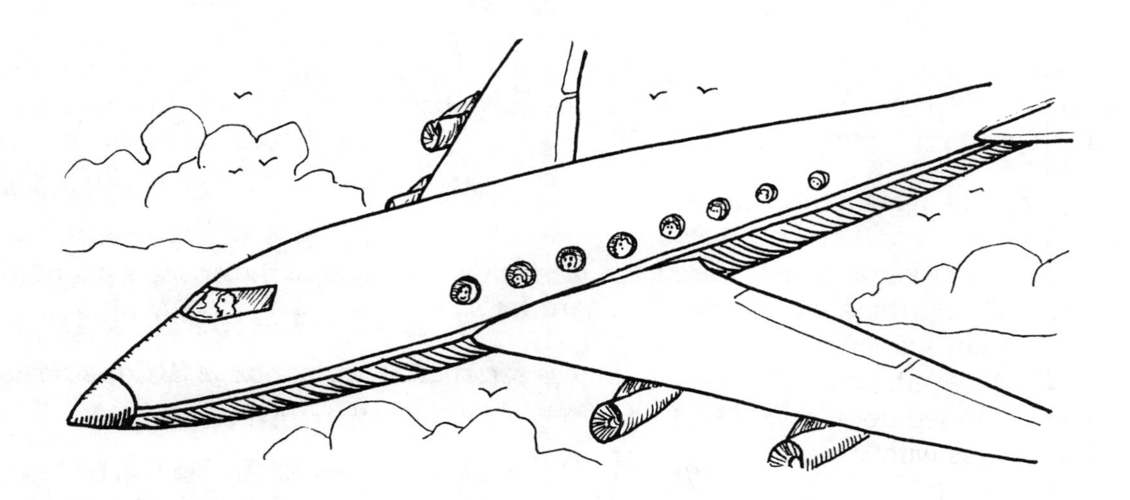

Objectives

- To contrast individual problem-solving efforts with those of a team.
- To discover the advantages and disadvantages in each.
- To illustrate that the "combined wisdom" advantage of group problem solving is sometimes the important consideration in comparing the two methods of problem solving.

Procedure

Organize the class into teams of five or six. You may want to consider the grouping by personality types instead of merely taking sections of the classroom as a team. First, distribute the three-page narrative titled "Basketball in the Snow" to each individual. Allow seven minutes for each student to read it and complete the assignment of classifying the 10 items in order of importance. (This is to simulate a sense of urgency in keeping with the situation in the story.) As soon as each student has completed his or her classification, have the team meet and develop a team ranking. Allow 10 minutes for this activity. Each student should have entered an individual ranking in column #1 of the second page. The team ranking should be placed in column #2.

When all of this is done, announce the "expert's" score and have the class record this in column #3 of their second page. To complete this activity, determine the *average* of the *individual scores.* You can gather the individual numbers for each item. Have someone in the class determine the average number by dividing the total number by the number of participants. When finished, determine the average of the team scores in the same way. Complete an additional "Scorecard" based upon comparing the averages with the expert ranking.

EXPERT RANKING

Rank	Item
6	*A mirror*
7	*A 9' rubber raft*
1	*A box of wooden matches*
10	*Five inflatable life jackets*
3	*A full can of kerosene*
4	*Seventy-five feet of rope*
2	*A canvas tent 10' x 10' x 8'*
5	*A small box with assorted knives and tools*
8	*A folding shovel*
9	*A compass*

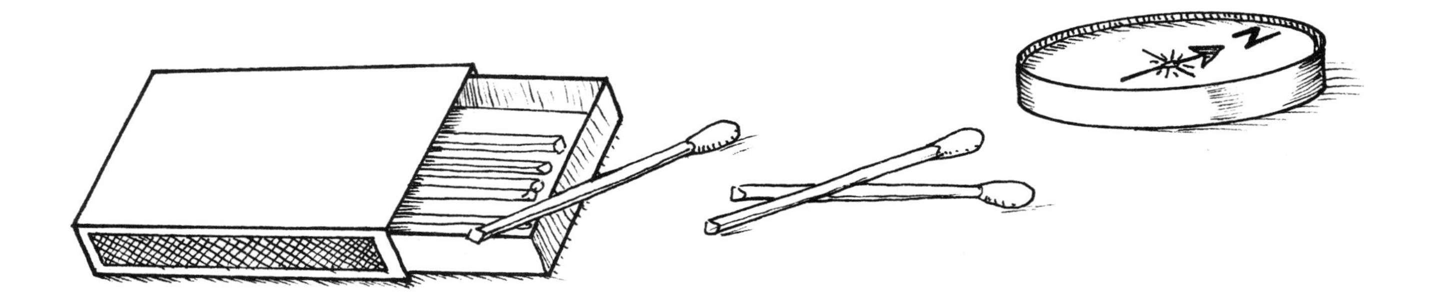

What to Expect

After individuals have read the narrative and made their choices, the group meetings might become quite active. This is because each individual will be trying to convince other team members that his/her choice is the right one. When there is disagreement in a group, have members vote and go with the consensus decision. Try to limit the time for this activity to encourage the idea that this is an urgent situation. If you sense that the activity is taking too much time, cut it short by announcing that there are only 60 seconds left.

Materials Required

Only copies of the student materials are necessary. You should keep an extra "Scorecard" to compile the average scores in the final group classification.

Approximate Time

The entire activity should last for approximately 45 minutes.

Discussion Questions

1. How do you justify the expert's choices?

(1) Matches–Obviously, in an ice and snow storm, it is important to keep people from freezing to death, especially those who are injured.

(2) Tent–In a storm, it is important to get people out of the wind and into a situation where heat can be generated and maintained.

(3) Kerosene–A fuel that will be important for keeping people warm. Healthy survivors can find kindling wood so that the kerosene is not used up too soon.

(4) Rope–Rope may be necessary for securing the tent in the wind or for helping in expanding the shelter.

(5) Tools–The knives and tools are necessary for getting more firewood and possibly expanding the shelter. For example, a "lean-to" may have to be constructed. The tools can be used to manipulate damaged plane parts as part of an expanded shelter.

(6) Mirror–This will be used to signal search planes.

(7) Raft–The raft may be useful for shelter or for dragging things or people to a better shelter. It can also be cut up and used for preparing a larger shelter.

(8) Shovel–Not too useful for digging holes but could be used as a paddle or part of a shelter.

(9) Compass–Since it is unlikely that the party will walk to safety, the compass will be of little use.

(10) Life Jackets–Of no value except as pillows in the tent. Anyone exposed to the cold lake water would quickly die.

2. Was there anything that came out of your team discussions that surprised you?

Students can bring out poor choices that they might have made. (For example, they may have thought the compass was more important than it was.)

3. How effective was your team? Could it have been more effective or efficient?

This is simply a way for individuals to evaluate the team effectiveness. Hopefully, some will recognize what it was that made their group work effectively or ineffectively. The following might be some of their reactions:

a. We could not agree on anything.

b. One or two people seemed to dominate the group and we could not get them to listen to others.

c. It was good because I heard good reasons for choices that I had not considered.

d. I liked the fact that I could contribute to the thinking of the group.

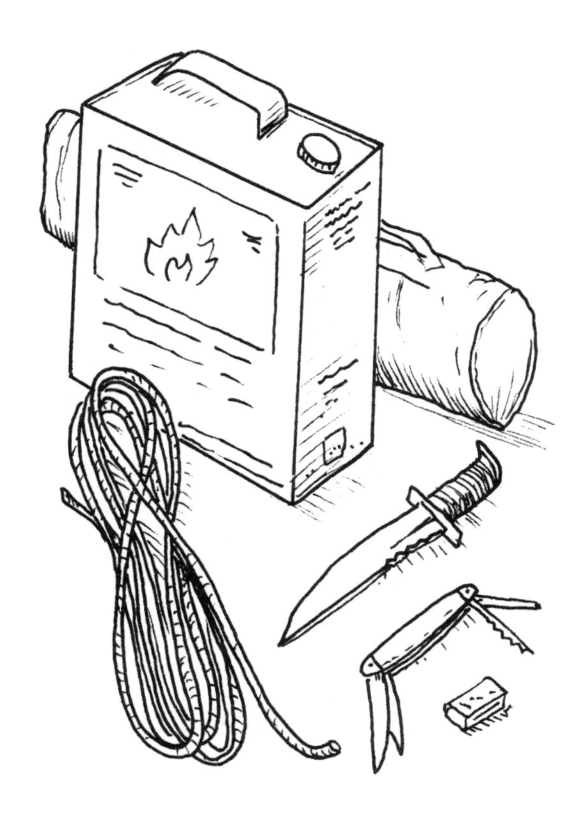

This activity is based upon one called "Alaskan Adventure," produced by Richard Hill of Effective Strategies, Inc., producers of Team Building Simulations materials and seminars. The corporation's address is:

Effective Strategies
2244 Loch Highland Drive
Dexter, MI 48130
1-800-874-2256

BASKETBALL IN THE SNOW

Your basketball team was selected to enter the prestigious tournament held in North Bay, Ontario. Only 16 teams in the United States are invited. This is a great opportunity for you, your school, and your community.

Business leaders from your community have arranged for the team, coaches, and some parents to charter two small planes to make the flight from Detroit, Michigan, to North Bay. The team will take one plane while the coaches and parents will take the other.

One hour into the flight, a serious storm develops. The radio in your plane is not working and the pilot realizes that she is being blown off course. The ice and snow reduce visibility to the point that you cannot see the front of the plane.

Suddenly, there is a small break in the weather and the pilot can see that she is perilously close to the ground but approaching a large, frozen lake. Although the team is terrified, they all agree that their best chances are to land on the frozen lake.

Although everyone is alive after the crash landing, your center has a broken leg. A minute before the plane explodes, you are able to salvage a few items from the cargo hold of the plane.

You must take immediate action to survive the harsh weather. You have five minutes to review the items that were salvaged from the plane. You are to classify them in order of importance for your survival. A *1* represents the most important item. A *10* represents the least important.

Name ____________________

SCORECARD

	You (1)	Team (2)	Expert (3)	You/ Expert (4)	Team/ Expert (5)
A mirror	___	___	___	___	___
A 9' rubber raft	___	___	___	___	___
A box of wooden matches	___	___	___	___	___
5 inflatable life jackets	___	___	___	___	___
A full can of kerosene	___	___	___	___	___
75' of rope	___	___	___	___	___
A canvas tent 10' x 10' x 8'	___	___	___	___	___
A box of knives and tools	___	___	___	___	___
A folding shovel	___	___	___	___	___
A compass	___	___	___	___	___
			Total	___	___

When you have completed your individual ranking, return to your group. Have the team agree on its own ranking. You may discuss your recommendations before agreeing on a choice. Enter the team choices in the appropriate column.

Once you have recorded the team score in your second column, your teacher will announce the expert score. Record it in column #3. Compare your score with the expert score by entering the numerical difference between the two in column #4. Add the numbers in this column and write the total at the bottom of the column. The smaller the number, the better your survival decisions.

Make the same comparison between your team and the expert by recording the difference between your team score and the expert score for each item. Then total the column. Your teacher will develop the average of all individual scores and team scores to make the final comparison and calculate your chances of survival in case of an emergency.

PULLING THE STRINGS

Objective

To illustrate the elements of effective team interaction:
(a) a clear purpose
(b) a plan
(c) clear roles
(d) ground rules

Procedure

First, the string, magic marker apparatus, and targets should be set and ready to use. This is explained in detail in the "Materials Required" section. A copy of the target should be made for each team that will be selected.

Select two teams of four or five members each. (You may find more dramatic results by "stacking the deck" and selecting four impulsive and excitable individuals for the first team. Select four or five more analytical and even-tempered people for the second team.) Explain to the first team that they are to control the magic marker by manipulating the four strings and place one mark in each of the 15 boxes on the target. The team will have five minutes to complete the task. If a line is touched on the target, a penalty will be assessed. If a string is broken or the marker comes loose, it must be repaired by the team, and they must start over. The team which has the highest score by placing marks in the most squares within the time limit wins.

Those not participating should be instructed to observe. Distribute the "Observer Instructions" to them and ask them to record their observations. They will be asked to evaluate each team. To begin, have the target, strings, and marker set up on the floor in a clear area of the classroom. Instruct the teams that they cannot pull too hard on the strings or the marker will come loose.

What to Expect

Depending on the makeup of each group, you will find that many interesting things will happen, for example:

1. If you have selected five people for the team, there will be a problem since there are only four ends of string. How this is resolved is interesting and will be discussed later.
2. Because each student in the group becomes so enthusiastic, each one behaves as an individual. This results in breaking the string, dislodging the marker, and frustration by others. Sometimes, individuals become so frustrated that they quit in disgust.
3. Sometimes, a group will carefully get used to their situation. They will learn how some must release pressure while others increase pressure to move the marker properly to achieve their goal. DO NOT TELL THEM THIS AHEAD OF TIME. THIS IS WHAT YOU WANT THE CLASS TO DISCOVER.
4. You may find that everyone wants a chance. You should stick with the plan of having two teams attempt the problem and follow this with a discussion. Then you may want to follow with more teams.

Materials Required

You will need to make a device consisting of two pieces of string that are each eight feet long, a magic marker, and a rubber band. Copies of the target should be given to each team.

The string is wrapped once around the magic marker in the center of the string and held in place by the rubber band. This is done with both strings.

The target is placed on the floor (over old newspapers) in the center of a circle of four students who are standing about eight feet apart from each other (see diagram). The magic marker should hover over the target and be lowered onto the target at the appropriate spots.

When you are ready, have students pick up the ends of the string, raise the marker off the floor, and remove the cap of the marker.

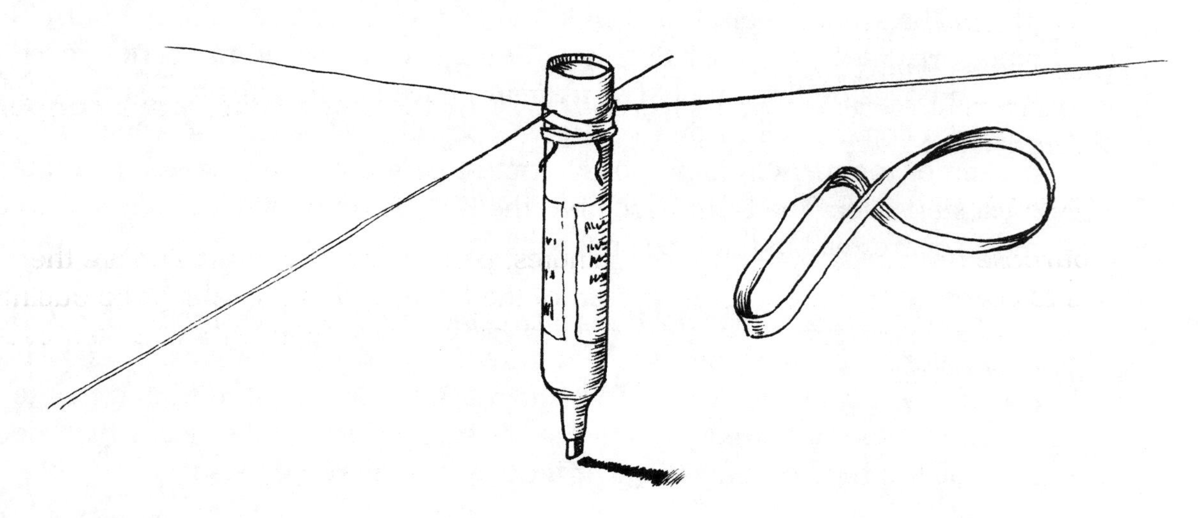

Approximate Time

One complete session should last about 45 minutes. If students want to continue the activity, save it for another day. You can actually conduct the same activity, along with the discussion, more than once. **Each team session should last exactly five minutes.**

Discussion Questions

1. **What was the difference between the teams that were successful (or the most successful) and those which were not?**

   Simply put, the teams where there was cooperation between the students holding the strings were probably the most successful. The least successful are usually those where each individual is trying to control the marker.

   Those team members who participated can discuss how they felt while they were playing the game.

2. **Does this activity illustrate the potential problems of any team activity (i.e., a basketball team or a team of people trying to recommend improvements in a school activity)?**

   Students should see the parallels between this activity and other types of team activities. A group behaving as individuals, with no purpose, no sense of belonging to a group, no plan, and a lack of cooperation generally fails.

3. **If a successful team is one in which the following four elements are clear, how does each apply to this activity?**
   a. **a clear purpose—the goal was clear, a mark in each box without touching the lines**
   b. **a plan—start with the big boxes**
   c. **clear roles—you release when I pull**
   d. **ground rules—everyone should not pull at the same time, work cooperatively taking your time, no yelling**

   In discussing each point, the following ideas should be brought out:

   The *purpose* is quite clear. Within five minutes, participants are to manipulate the strings to control a marker and touch each of the boxes without touching the outlines. The purpose is so clear that participants usually stumble through without a plan because the outcome seems so obvious.

The successful teams will usually evolve a *plan*. They will recognize that all four strings cannot be pulled. They will begin giving instructions for some to add pressure and others to release. They will discuss which boxes to attack first. Unsuccessful teams will not get to this stage.

Usually, definite *roles* can be seen during this activity. Who took control at the beginning of the activity? Did someone else take charge later? What was the role of the fifth person? The best use of this person would be to give instructions to others.

For the team to be successful, certain *ground rules* had to evolve. In a successful team, you cannot have someone who gets mad and quits. It is not helpful to have someone criticizing someone else in the group. In this particular activity, you cannot pull too hard on the strings.

Follow Up

You may get requests to repeat this activity since the experience gained convinces everyone that they could be successful a second time. You may try to set it up with someone given the role of manager who instructs the four "string holders."

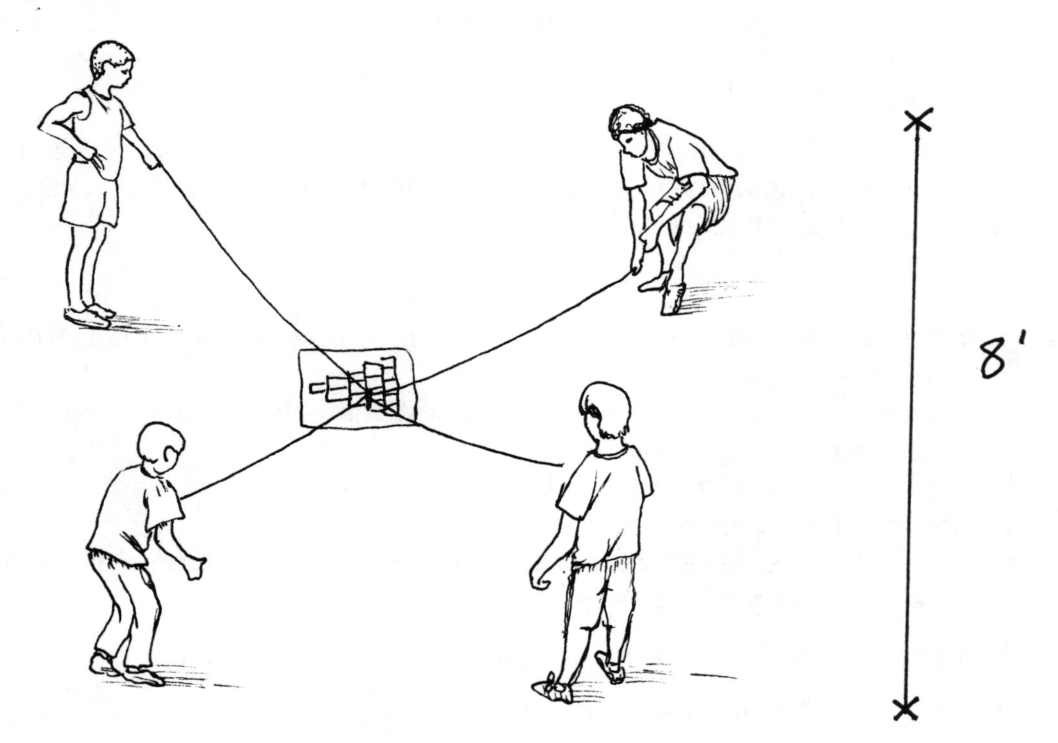

SOURCE: This activity is based on a learning simulation designed and developed by Interel, San Francisco, CA and used in team building workshops developed by Tom Noonan, Paragon Alliance, Inc., 7639 Whitehall Circle East, West Chester, OH, 45069. Paragon Alliance is an international firm specializing in Team Performance and Strategic Planning.

Name ______________________________

PULLING THE STRINGS

TEAM INSTRUCTIONS:
Control the magic marker by holding the string at each end and place a mark in as many boxes as possible within five minutes. All marks must be placed within the boxes and not touch the borders of the boxes. Count the value of each box in which a mark was placed correctly. Subtract twice the value of the box with the highest number in which a line (border) was touched.

If you can place one mark correctly in boxes 11 through 15 you will receive 25 bonus points.

TEAM SCORE:
After the end of the five-minute team session, enter the numbers within the boxes that were marked correctly. In the right column, enter the penalty points resulting from touching the lines. (Remember, the penalty is subtracting the highest number.) Add bonus points, if appropriate, and calculate your team score.

POINTS	PENALTY	BONUS
______	______	
______	______	
______	______	
______	______	
______	______	
______	______	
______	______	
______	______	
______	______	
______	______	
______	______	
______	______	
______	______	
______	______	______
______	______	______
______	______	______

Totals ______ (-) ______ (+) ______ = TEAM SCORE______

Name________________________________

OBSERVER INSTRUCTIONS:

Watch the teams attempt to score on the target placed on the floor. Your job is to determine what made each team successful or unsuccessful. To help in the process, record your notes in the appropriate areas below:

THINGS WHICH MADE THE GROUP

SUCCESSFUL	UNSUCCESSFUL
____________________	____________________
____________________	____________________
____________________	____________________
____________________	____________________
____________________	____________________
____________________	____________________
____________________	____________________
____________________	____________________
____________________	____________________
____________________	____________________
____________________	____________________
____________________	____________________
____________________	____________________
____________________	____________________
____________________	____________________
____________________	____________________
____________________	____________________
____________________	____________________
____________________	____________________
____________________	____________________
____________________	____________________
____________________	____________________
____________________	____________________
____________________	____________________
____________________	____________________
____________________	____________________

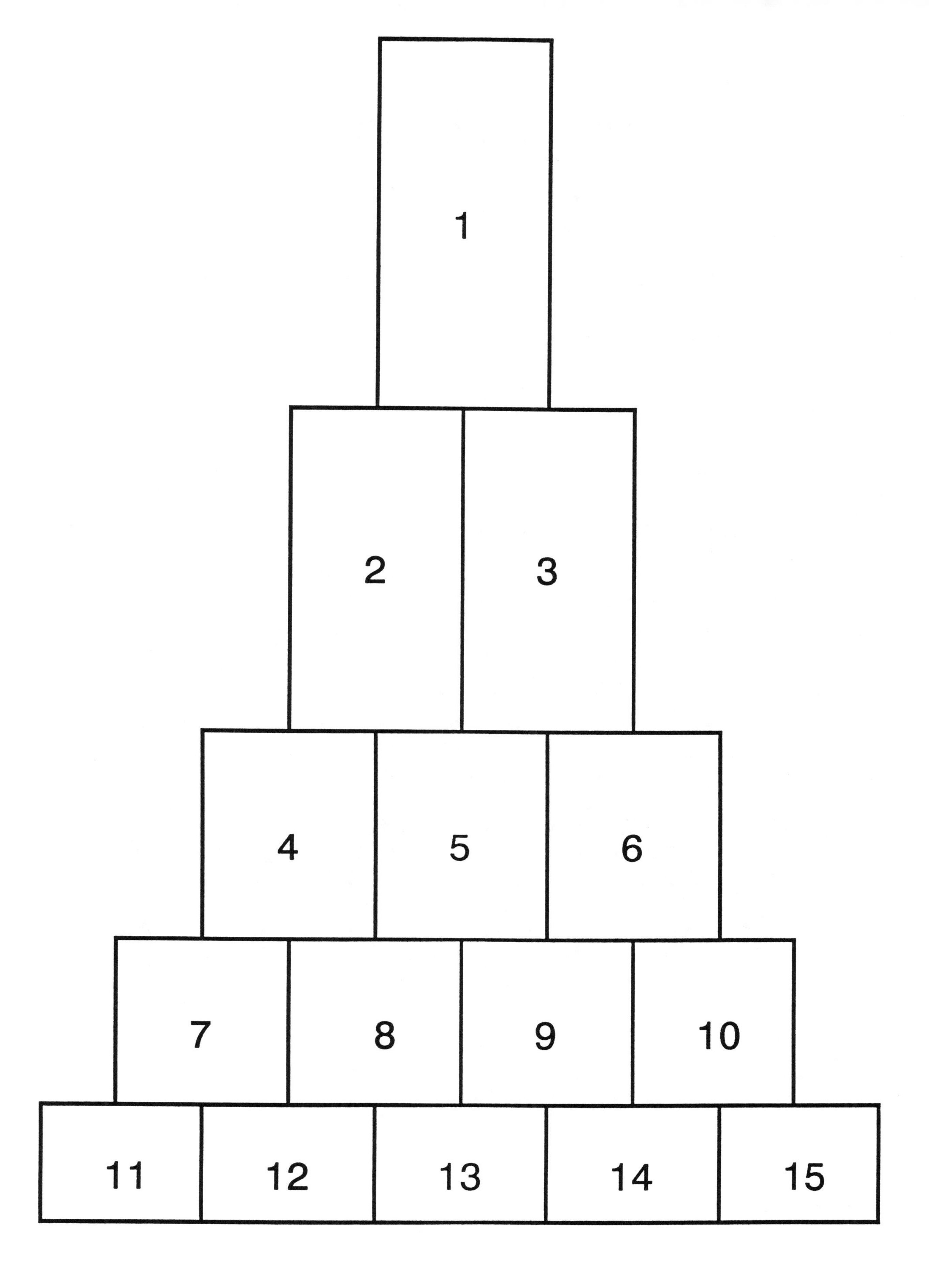
1
2
3
4
5
6
7
8
9
10
11
12
13
14
15

MISSION IMPOSSIBLE

Objective

Given a description of a variety of personality types, students shall select the four they feel would be the most appropriate for their team. The team's assignment is to invent an educational game based on the format of Bingo. Students shall gradually discover that certain types of behavior are appropriate (and inappropriate) at certain stages of problem solving. Those stages are

1. Problem Definition
2. Data Gathering
3. Idea Generation
4. Idea Selection
5. Implementation

Procedure

Distribute copies of the student materials and ask students to read the first page "Good morning." Explain that they are to assume that they are to follow a specific procedure with their team to solve the problem described in the mission. They are to review the backgrounds of a group of individuals from which to select four as members of their team.

The class is to read the background information which describes the process to be used. Students can think of this process as the focus of five team meetings during which a specific agenda is followed. For example, the first meeting is to establish the mission and assign fact-finding assignments. The second will review the fact-finding results and assign each group member to develop ideas.

What to Expect

Hopefully, students will select individuals who are best suited for the assignment. Furthermore, they might define a useful role for everyone but understand that certain types of behavior are appropriate for certain stages of problem solving. They should discover which behaviors and general traits are appropriate at the various stages of problem solving. Students can also generalize about team effectiveness when too many of a particular type of person are on a team.

Materials Required

Each class member should receive copies of the student materials. No other materials are required for this activity.

Approximate Time	The activity has been designed to take 30 to 40 minutes depending upon the level of class discussion. NOTE: The activity called "BINGO" is intended to follow this one.

Discussion Questions

1. Whom did you select for your team and why did you select them?

Listen to student selections and their reasoning for their choices. If you observe that several students made the same choices, try to determine the qualities of the people who were frequently selected. (This discussion could take 5 to 15 minutes.)

2. Which individuals do you think are best suited for each stage of the process?

Make up a grid chart on the chalkboard listing the five stages as columns and the names of the people as rows. Ask the class to arrive at a numerical rating for each person for each stage. Rate on a scale of 1 to 10 with 10 representing ideal. What follows is an example:

	Define	Fact	Idea	Select	Implement
Booker	7	7	2	7	5
Peggy	6	5	5	7	7
Dora	5	8	4	6	10
Melvin	6	6	4	6	9
Alice	10	9	10	9	5
Ben	5	8	5	5	7
Gilda	8	5	8	7	8
Warren	4	4	3	6	5
Anno	5	7	2	6	6

Ask the class to give reasons for their ratings and to select four people. For example, Alice is important for helping develop good ideas, Dora will be necessary to finish the project, Gilda will be able to contribute in all areas, and Ben could serve several purposes, especially in the areas of research and fact finding.

3. What might happen if such a team were made up of four people exactly like

(a) Alice? You may get a great deal of ideas and plans but they may not be completed because of lack of interest in the "nitty gritty" details of producing the materials.

(b) Ben? You may not get any ideas. Unless someone told them what to do, nothing would get done.

(c) Anno? Nothing would happen; they would simply argue and never stick to the point.

Remember, the point is not to classify people as able or unable, but to realize that the chances of success are greater if you choose people who are appropriate for the task. You should emphasize that real people have to play many roles and that we are not condemned to accept only one.

Name________________________________

MISSION IMPOSSIBLE

Good Morning.

Your mission, should you choose to accept it, is to form a team of five individuals (including you) and invent a game that can be used in your classroom. The game must be in the same format as Bingo and be useful in learning or practicing skills in mathematics, geography, science, or social studies.

What follows are two briefing papers. Study each since they clarify the rest of your mission.

GOOD LUCK!

FOR YOUR EYES ONLY
BACKGROUND INFORMATION

The first element in your briefing is to understand the process that will be used by your team. It is a series of stages or specific things that your team will do to fulfill the mission successfully.

Your team assignment will involve a five-stage operation. First, your team should **define the problem.** In this case defining the problem is the mission statement listed earlier. It is important that all team members understand clearly what they are trying to do. What is the outcome to be?

The second step may require **data or fact finding**. In order to develop a satisfactory solution and implement it, there may be things you simply need to know. For example, does anyone know how Bingo is played? How do you win at Bingo? What kinds of math, geography, science, or social science learning might fit into this format? How many squares are on a Bingo card?

Once you know what you need to know, it is appropriate to create as many ideas as you can over a specific period of time. This is called the **idea generation** stage. If you want your team to have a good idea, develop lots of them. See if your team can generate at least 10 to 15 ideas.

Since all individuals on the team may not agree on the best idea, it may be necessary to select a fair procedure to evaluate and select your best idea. This is the process of **idea selection.** This will be your team's solution to your problem.

Finally, your team must **implement** the idea. In this case, the difficult process of developing written materials, rules, and boards must be completed. Last-minute problems have to be resolved. Often, there is a deadline to be met.

Knowing the mission and the process your team should go through, continue to the next briefing.

FOR YOUR EYES ONLY

The second part of the briefing explains some background about the people available for you to select as members on this mission. Based upon your understanding of the mission, and the process that you should go through, select from the following list the four people who would be the most appropriate in developing a satisfactory solution. Again, good luck.

CANDIDATE PROFILES

Booker Van Wormer

Our agents have learned that Booker is a smart kid. Friends say that he typically studies situations carefully before making up his mind. He is slow to "jump onto the bandwagon," preferring instead to review the situation from many angles. Because of this, he often seems aloof and not much of a "joiner" or "team player."

Most people feel that Booker is a little boring, but they wish they had his ability.

Peggy Poplar

Everyone likes Peggy. She dresses well and looks good. She is popular because she is typically encouraging and positive to others. Those who do not like her feel that all she can do is talk and show sympathy for others.

Our investigation has concluded that Peggy is a diplomat, with an ability to get groups of people to agree on things. We have also concluded that she does not easily make decisions on her own nor take a strong position on issues.

Dora Dunn

They say that Dora Dunn lives to solve complex problems. When all else fails, Dora will take your problem and make sense out of it. She hates being in the spotlight but likes being close to it. She is active in the drama club but only in behind-the-scenes work, such as working with makeup, props, and other tasks.

Dora always finishes what she starts. Many kids in school talk about things, others like to start projects, but Dora likes to finish them.

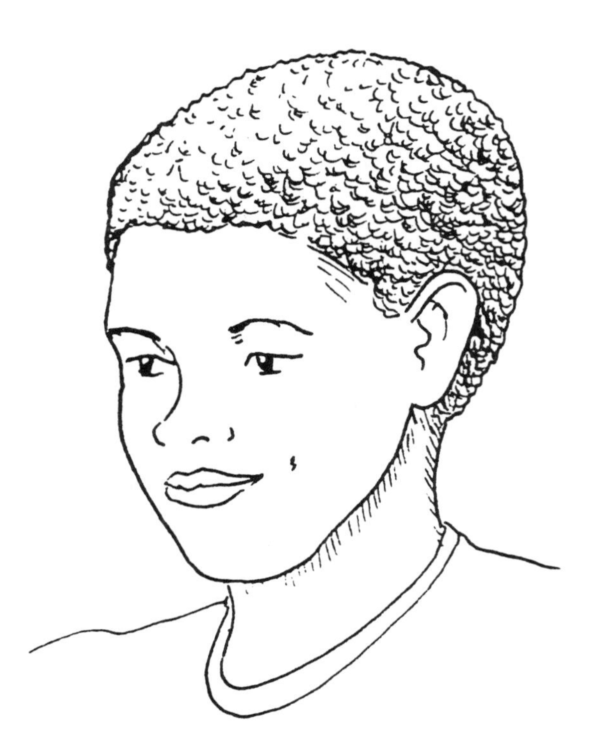

Melvin Works

Melvin has a gift. He can turn other people's trash into something useful. He is what school counselors call "mechanically inclined." He amazes others with his patience and ability to figure out "what goes where."

Although Melvin is good at things that he knows, he does not like anything that he does not understand. For example, give him a broken-down car and he will have it running in "no time." Ask him to create something else and he could not be bothered.

Alice Einstein

Our research shows that Alice is considered an "odd-ball" by some of her classmates. When asked why they feel this way, students reported that Alice does not dress in the same manner as others, nor is she interested in the same things as the other kids her age.

Alice hates being criticized and loves praise. Her interests are in designing her own clothes, art, and those activities which require new ideas and ventures.

Ben Blabby

Ben is blessed with "the gift of gab." He could talk a polar bear into buying a winter coat. Wherever Ben goes, enthusiasm goes with him. "Blab," as his friends call him, is a good listener and is usually interested in everything with which he is involved. This interest tends to spread to those around him. Ben is happiest when he is doing highly structured things. This way, he does not have to think about them.

Gilda Gogetter

Our information on Gilda reveals a pleasant person with a lot of friends. Friends report that she is liked because she is quick to praise and encourage others. She is slow to anger and is usually quite even-tempered.

Gilda is president of the student council and captain of the girls' volleyball team. When she was in the seventh grade, she started a baby-sitting business. She recruited 10 friends to work for her. She lined up 5 to 10 jobs per week, trained her friends on how to be great baby-sitters and charged her customers $2.00 per hour. She paid her sitters $1.00 per hour. Today she schedules 35 baby-sitters each week.

In our interview with Gilda she stated that she was neither smart nor talented. Her grades in school are somewhat above average.

Warren Wonderful

Warren is a starter on both the soccer and hockey teams. He is a true "rah rah" type guy. He is the type of person who gets what he wants by bullying his way through situations.

Warren shows interest in things but can easily become bored. While he is interested, he will move mountains. When he loses interest, you will not see him.

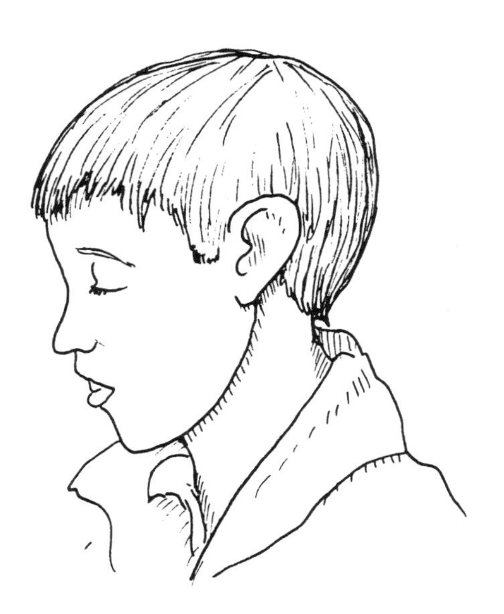

Anno Ying

Anno is probably the smartest kid in school. He knows more about anything than anyone you know. That's the good news. The bad news is that he is argumentative, condescending, and talks too much. He appears to take joy in criticizing others.

His science teachers cannot remember the last time he missed a question on a test.

BINGO

Objectives

- To invent an instructional game using the Bingo format.
- To utilize a team selection process whereby decisions can be made on an objective basis.

Procedure

Divide the class into teams of four or more. Instruct each team to select a chairperson. It will be his or her responsibility to manage the team through the end of this activity. NOTE: After today's activity, two to three more team meetings will be necessary to complete the assignment. Hopefully, teams will call their meetings on their own time. If they do not, you may have to allow for team meetings over the next two weeks.

Distribute the first page of the student materials to the chairpersons of each team. They are to read these instructions to their teams. When this is completed, you are to assign each team a discipline. Use the following disciplines:

MATHEMATICS GEOGRAPHY SCIENCE HISTORY

If you want to add some mystery, write these disciplines on cards and let someone from each team select a card. There should be as many cards as there are teams.

After teams have reviewed instructions, make sure that they understand the desired result—a Bingo game which provides or reinforces learning in a subject using a Bingo format. Part of each team's responsibility is to discover ways to use this format for reinforcing learning in a particular subject. The following page illustrates a variety of possibilities. (Do not recommend anything unless the team is unable to make a connection between the Bingo format and some type of subject matter.)

The result will be a series of Bingo cards (each of which is different from the others) and a set of questions. There should be about 50 questions for each game. For example, a game could be developed for learning the capitals of the 50 states.

CAPITALS

B	I	N	G	O
Lansing				
		WILD		

Use U.S. Capitals

SPANISH

B	I	N	G	O
Madrid	Bueno			
Mañana				
		WILD		

Use Vocabulary Words

MATH

B	I	N	G	O
27				
81				
144	101	WILD		
16	99			

Use Answers to Problems

MATH

B	I	N	G	O
$(X+3) = 5$				
		WILD		

Use Answers to Problems

HISTORY

B	I	N	G	O
1492				
		WILD		

Important Events

CIVICS

B	I	N	G	O
Brown vs. Bd. of Ed.				
Search and Seizure				
		WILD		

Court Decisions, Bill of Rights

Each Bingo card would list 24 state capitals. The 50 questions would simply ask the names of the states. Players would have to know the names of the capital cities and mark them off on their Bingo cards.

Distribute the remaining pages to the team members. Have the chairperson assign each team member a role (i.e., inventor, fact finder). Each student should be prepared to report or complete a task for the next in a series of meetings. These meetings can be scheduled at this time.

Review the Idea Selection section before the team is ready to choose its project from the list of ideas prepared by the inventor(s). This section illustrates one of many methods for groups to select their choices while taking into consideration the feelings of each individual in the team (see student materials).

What to Expect

Ideally, each team will find this an interesting project. If a team calls its own meetings and tries to keep the result a secret until the project is due, your mission will have been accomplished.

If some teams have trouble, assist them by reinforcing team roles or answering their questions.

Some may think that they will need Ping-Pong balls (which are sometimes used at local Bingo games). You can suggest (and provide) 3" x 5" cards for the questions.

Probably every team should ask about the master control sheet. This is a grid which lists all of the answers available on all of the cards. After the announcer for each game reads a question, he or she places a mark over its answer. This is done to validate the cards of winners and make sure that they have not marked an incorrect answer.

Discussion Questions

The "proof of the pudding" will come in playing the Bingo games. The Bingo games not only reinforce learning in your class, but can be used in other classes as well. When they are used in other classes, a great deal of enthusiasm is generated toward you and your students. The highest form of flattery (and a cause for self-confidence) is experienced when something that is used and enjoyed by others is created.

1. Did anyone have difficulty fulfilling the role that he/she assumed in his/her team?

Let students ventilate their feelings. Try to get them to discover that we all play many roles. We are better at some than others, but sometimes we are asked to play a role because there is no one else who can assume it.

2. Explain why you think your team had such an easy/difficult time on this project.

There can be a variety of reasons on each side. The most interesting discussions might be about success. The reason was probably that individuals were able to assume roles assigned and carry them out.

3. Can you think of any other ways of creating learning games using the Bingo format?

Again, allow time to discuss this. From a problem-solving point of view this is valuable thinking. It requires the individual to view two disparate topics and see a way of connecting them.

IF ONE OR MORE GAMES WERE INVENTED, CONGRATULATIONS TO YOU. YOUR CLASSROOM ATMOSPHERE IS ONE IN WHICH STUDENTS CAN EXERCISE THE HIGHEST FORM OF COGNITIVE ACTIVITY . . . CREATING.

BINGO

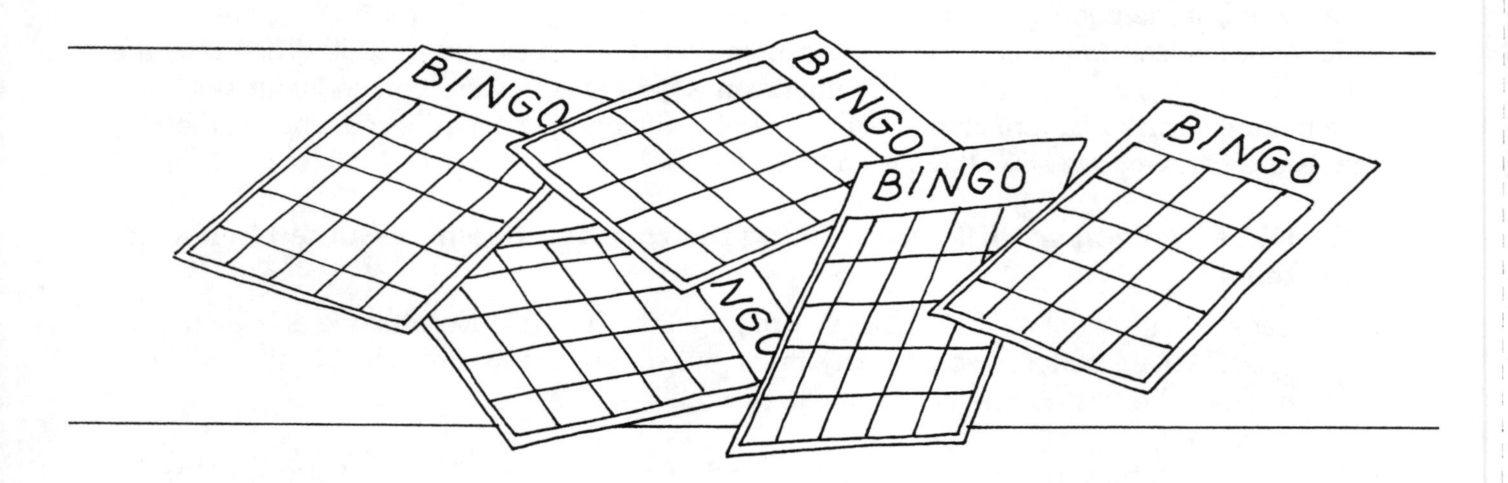

Your team has been assigned the task of inventing a learning game. The game is to be based upon the Bingo format. Your team will be required to meet several times, and you will be asked to play a special role. The result should be a game that can be played by your class (or others) as a way of learning or reinforcing learning in a particular subject area. The following is an outline of things to be done at each of your next four meetings. You will be asked to play a particular role in developing a solution and in implementing your solution.

TEAM INSTRUCTIONS:

1. At your first meeting, elect a chairperson. It will be this person's responsibility to call and moderate meetings.

2. Your teacher will assign you a subject (math, science, or geography). In addition, the newly elected chairperson will provide each team member with a role assignment which outlines tasks to be completed prior to your second meeting.These roles can be assigned to more than one person.

3. Your final product will be a set of Bingo cards, a set of questions, and a master control sheet. Completed games can be tested in your classroom and made available to other schools and classrooms.

ROLES:

1. **CHAIRPERSON:** You are to assign the roles to members of your team. If there are more people than roles, assign the same role to more than one person. Your goal is that all tasks (roles) are assigned and completed for the meetings that you will lead. You may assign yourself a role after each team member has received his/her assignment.

   Call the next meeting of your team. Give your Fact Finder time to complete his or her task. The meeting can be anytime (lunch, after school).

2. **FACT FINDER:** It is your job to learn as much about the game of Bingo as you can. You must be able to explain the game to your team by the second meeting. The better you understand the game and the better you can communicate this to your team, the better your results will be. This is an important role.

3. **INVENTOR:** It will be your task to think of eight or more ideas for Bingo games. You will be assigned a discipline by your teacher (math, geography, etc.).

4. **IMPLEMENTOR:** Once your team has developed its plan, it will be your job to carry it out. You are to make the Bingo cards, question cards, and a master control sheet. Other members of your team may help you in this task, but you are the boss.

SCHEDULE:

Meeting #1: Elect a chairperson, assign roles, schedule your next meeting, and receive a certain discipline from your teacher.

Meeting #2: Fact-finder report, questions, discussion of possibilities.

Meeting #3: Inventor reports on eight possibilities; the group discusses and selects a final project. Implementor assigns each team member an even number of questions to complete overnight (if necessary).

Meeting #4: Implementor displays completed Bingo cards, question cards, and master control sheet.

IDEA SELECTION:

A useful tool for teams when deciding on a course of action is the weighted voting technique. In Meeting #3, the team is asked to select its choice of eight or more ideas. To do this, ask each team member to write each idea on a sheet of paper. They are then to give weighted values to their choices by using a 10-point total with no single idea receiving over 5 points. Not every idea has to be selected. Below are examples of this method of assigning values to choices.

	Vote 1	Vote 2	Vote 3	Vote 4	Total
Idea #1	1		2	1	4
Idea #2		2	2	1	5
Idea #3	5	3	2	3	13
Idea #4	2	2		1	5
Idea #5	2	1	2	1	6
Idea #6		1		2	3
Idea #7		1	1	1	3
Idea #8			1		1
	10	**10**	**10**	**10**	**40**

You can see that Idea #3 was the clear choice of the team and that #5 was the second choice.

B I N G O

B	I	N	G	O
		WILD		

TWO EARS BUT ONE MOUTH

Objectives

- To illustrate the difficulty in being an empathic listener.
- To provide a vehicle for practicing the skill of listening as a way of better understanding the thoughts, views, and opinions of others to arrive at a solution satisfactory to all.

Procedure

Arrange the class into teams of four students each. Students should sit in teams. Each team will be asked to discuss ideas for a school project. A different "Character Card" should be distributed to each team member.

The Character Card is to be completed by each team member before beginning the activity. This will require two or three minutes. STUDENTS SHOULD NOT SHARE THEIR CHARACTER DESCRIPTIONS WITH ANYONE UNTIL THE ENTIRE ACTIVITY IS COMPLETE.

The Character Cards list information about the individual that he or she is to reveal during the discussion. At the end of the activity, you will surprise the students by asking them to recount information about their team members instead of ideas about the project.

The first part of the activity requires students to complete some of the information on their character cards. If a question seems inappropriate, they should simply make up an answer. Once the character cards have been completed, ask each team to spend 15 or 20 minutes reviewing this question: "In what ways might the school design, fund, and construct a greenhouse so that students might conduct research in biology?"

What to Expect

Hopefully, students will discuss the "greenhouse project." It may seem a little artificial since students are trying to disclose the information about themselves from the "Character Cards." Some students may "smell a rat" and realize that this might be a setup. If so, simply encourage them to develop good ideas about the greenhouse project.

Procedure

When you feel the teams are running out of steam, stop the meetings. Announce that to complete this activity, each team member will be asked to recount the position of another team member, as follows:

Character #1 describes Character #3
Character #3 describes Character #4
Character #4 describes Character #2
Character #2 describes Character #1

When describing another character, students are to recall five pieces of personal information about the person and how he or she might best contribute to the greenhouse problem. The character being described should keep score by checking off items from his or her character cards that were recalled. Later, students will be asked to give the score of the person who had to do the remembering.

Allow two minutes for each person to describe the comments of another team member. This will require that each team member recount the comments of another.

What to Expect

This might get a little noisy. Many people will be embarrassed that they cannot remember many of the details of the comments of a team member. THIS IS IMPORTANT, SINCE THEY MUST DISCOVER THAT THEY MAY NOT BE GOOD LISTENERS.

Approximate Time

This activity should take approximately one hour.

Materials Required

Only copies of the student materials are required.

Discussion Questions

1. **Ask for a show of hands from students who had a score of two or less.**

   (Meaning, the person who recounted input could remember only no more than two items that they mentioned during the discussions).

   Three items?

   Four items?

   Five items?

2. **Why do you think so many people could not remember what other people said during the team discussions?**

   If people are honest, they will probably say that they were too busy thinking of what they wanted to say instead of listening to others.

3. **What do you think would be the advantage in your understanding each team member's position as well as they do?**

   This is the point of the activity. Hopefully students will realize that by understanding the background and ideas of others, better decisions can be made which satisfy everyone. In addition, people become more enthusiastic about contributing to improvements when they have input into the process.

CHARACTER CARD #1

During the team meeting, it is important that the other members of your team know the following information about you. Fill in the blank lines with specific information about yourself. If something does not apply to you, make something up.

_____ 1. Your middle name is ____________________________. It is from a famous uncle in your family who invented the _________________.

_____ 2. You would be interested in designing the greenhouse since you have had some experience in designing simple structures.

_____ 3. Last year you were elected _______________ of your class at your school in _____________________ *(list city in which you lived)*.

_____ 4. Your older brother is a minor league ball player.

_____ 5. You would like to see the greenhouse located _________________________ ________________________ *(List somewhere on school property.)*

_____ 6. ____
____

(Make up something that you want your group to know about you.)

CHARACTER CARD #2

During the team meeting, it is important that the other members of your team know the following information about you. Fill in the blank lines with specific information about yourself. If something does not apply to you, make something up.

_____ 1. You are originally from ____________________*(list big city)* and think this is a "hick" town.

_____ 2. You would be interested in building the greenhouse since you have had some experience in construction.

_____ 3. Last year you won an award for __________________ on the __________________ team.

_____ 4. Your best friend made a commercial which will be seen on local television.

_____ 5. You would like to see the greenhouse located on the south side of the building where it will get the most sun.

_____ 6. ____

____

(Make up something that you want your group to know about you.)

CHARACTER CARD #3

During the team meeting, it is important that the other members of your team know the following information about you. Fill in the blank lines with specific information about yourself. If something does not apply to you, make something up.

_____ 1. You have been told that you look a lot like a famous ____________________ who is seen on the TV show ____________________.

_____ 2. You would be interested in working in the greenhouse since you have a lot of ideas for experiments with plants.

_____ 3. You are a strong believer in pyramid power. You believe that there is some mystical power in the shape of the ancient pyramids and that this power can be helpful to things placed within a pyramid.

_____ 4. You won a blue ribbon last year in the 50-yard dash.

_____ 5. You would like to see the greenhouse located ____________________. *(List somewhere on school property.)*

_____ 6. ____

____

(Make up something that you want your group to know about you.)

CHARACTER CARD #4

During the team meeting, it is important that the other members of your team know the following information about you. Fill in the blank lines with specific information about yourself. If something does not apply to you, make something up.

_____ 1. You find your teacher's tests easy since choice "B" in the multiple choice questions is always the correct answer.

_____ 2. You would be interested in getting people from the community to contribute money to finance construction of the greenhouse. You enjoy doing these kinds of things.

_____ 3. You hate the school lunches. You would prefer to grow vegetables in a school garden and serve them for school lunches. You would like to start a project where school food is provided by students who grow and sell food to the school.

_____ 4. You are a chocolate fanatic. You will eat anything as long as there is chocolate on it.

_____ 5. You would like to see a series of greenhouses and gardens located on property near the school and tended by students.

_____ 6. ____

____

(Make up something that you want your group to know about you.)

WHAT DO YOU DO WHEN THE BOTTOM DROPS OUT?

Objective

To desensitize students from behaving poorly in team activities by portraying the common problems associated with teams and illustrating their negative effects. Realizing that teams will often have difficulty in working effectively, anticipate the common problems associated with team dynamics and consider methods of overcoming them.

Procedure

Begin by asking students what kinds of things hinder effective team interaction. Let them suggest some of the problems they have encountered.

Distribute the student handout which lists eight of the common problems encountered in team situations and ask them to write one thing they might do, as the team chairperson, to overcome the problems.

In addition to sharing solutions as a class, the discussion questions will suggest solutions to be considered.

What to Expect

Students may mention problems that are not included in their activity. Add them to the list. Hopefully, many of the items mentioned will have been mentioned in the preliminary discussions.

Materials Required

Only copies of the student reading are required.

Approximate Time

The entire activity should last about an hour. If there is good discussion, it may take longer, or a follow-up could be scheduled to complete the discussions in a later activity.

Discussion Questions

For each of the following, allow students to read their written responses and discuss each item. The comments listed are points that should be made.

1. **You just cannot get going.**

   Have each team member write his or her ideas. Discuss what each has written. See if a plan can be developed by combining ideas. Make sure everyone understands what the problem (or mission) is.

2. **The team bully intimidates others.**

   Attempt to get agreement that the thoughts of everyone must be considered. Remember the early activities ("Basketball in the Snow" and "Lost on the Sixth Moon in the Justinian System") where it was proven that the combination of individuals' ideas was better than those of individuals. Stress the courage to do the right thing instead of being dominated in your thinking.

3. **Some members do not contribute.**

   Make sure that each member has an assigned role. Change these roles if some simply cannot follow them. Arrange to divide your team into subgroups so that the reluctant team members might focus upon something that they can do.

4. **Everybody believes the first thing they hear.**

   Often, everyone jumps on the first bandwagon they see. Agree to leave ideas on the shelf while searching for better ideas or solutions. It is comfortable to know you can always return to that first one. Attempt to go through a phase where ideas and procedures are challenged. You simply want to make sure you are not settling for an average plan when a great one may be "just around the corner."

5. **Some just want to get it over with.**

   Sometimes the goal gets confused and people become more concerned about being the first to finish than about solving the problem. Remind the class of those students who delight in finishing the tests early. Remind them that a grade is usually for quality, not speed.

6. Is this good enough?

This attitude suggests people who want to please others even if they have not done their best work. Remind everyone that they should try to satisfy themselves. When you ask this question, it suggests that you know it is not good enough but hope that someone else will.

7. Too many scatterbrains.

When some on the team cannot focus, plan future team meetings with very specific tasks for these people. They will find it easier to contribute. Plan each meeting with a specific start and finish so that everyone knows exactly what to expect.

8. Preserving the peace.

It is not uncommon to work closely with someone you do not like. You must convince people that their effectiveness cannot depend upon others. It is like believing that you can function only when conditions are favorable. Get in the habit of giving your best effort no matter what conditions prevail. If team members distract the meetings, get them to settle their disputes on their own time. As team leader, attempt to settle the dispute.

Make it clear that all of these things are easier "said than done." Nevertheless, this is what leadership is all about.

Author's Note: All people with a serious interest in team dynamics are indebted to Dr. Brian L. Joiner, a leader in the worldwide quality movement. If faculty groups are involved in team training as a way of improving their schools, methods of operation, and learning the use of a new set of tools, get and use *The Team Handbook,* by Joiner Associates, Inc. This activity was inspired by this book. Many of the significant improvements in the American Quality Movement have also been inspired by Joiner.

Name ______________________________

WHAT DO YOU DO WHEN THE BOTTOM DROPS OUT?

Getting teams to work effectively can sometimes be difficult. Since you will often be called upon to manage a team, it is helpful to know how to keep it focused and able to effectively complete its task. Below are listed eight things that sometimes happen in team activities. You will be asked to write one thing that you would do to overcome each problem so that you can get a variety of ideas.

Write one thing you would do to overcome each problem.

1. You just cannot get going. The team has no ideas or ability to develop a plan.

   ____

   ____

2. The team "bully" intimidates others to follow his/her ideas.

   ____

   ____

3. Some members just do not contribute.

   ____

   ____

Name ______________________________

4. Everybody believes the first thing they hear. They are not willing to reach for better solutions or test their assumptions.

____

____

5. Some people just want to "get it over with." They believe that completion, even when it is uninspired, is better than looking for better ideas.

____

____

6. Is this good enough? The whole group is content to be ordinary.

____

____

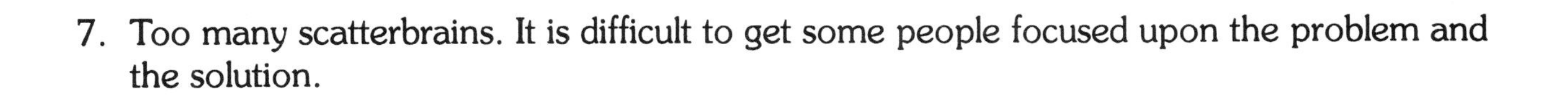

7. Too many scatterbrains. It is difficult to get some people focused upon the problem and the solution.

____

____

8. Preserving the peace. Sometimes two people on a team simply do not like each other.

____

____

HARDLY HERALDRY

Objective

To begin establishing a sense of continuity among a group of classroom teams by focusing upon their views of their own individual and collective identities. Using a short background in heraldry, develop a team "Coat of Arms" which will be associated with that team for later classroom activities and projects.

Procedure

Divide the class into teams of four or five members. Consider the "group chemistry" carefully, attempting to have a good variety of the personality types such as those described in "Mission Impossible." You can announce the following as an introduction to this activity:

You will be assigned to action teams that will be responsible for developing some interesting projects and solving problems. Later activities will be handled by the teams that are formed today.

To begin, you will be asked to establish a coat of arms for your team as a way of establishing a team identity. (If you were a hockey team, you would be designing the logo for your jersey.)

After reading the materials on heraldry, individuals should proceed to the steps. After completing the six steps individually, the team should meet to develop a consensus of the qualities that will be reflected in a team coat of arms and decide how to visualize them.

Distribute copies of the coat of arms to each individual along with an extra that can be used by the team.

Allow each team 10 to 15 minutes to decide on how their coat of arms will appear. Ask each group to assign one or more members to prepare a drawing in the blank that can be presented to the group. In addition, assign someone in each group to take the sample home and prepare a finished product, complete with colors and lettering.

What to Expect

Hopefully, teams will think more expansively than the lesson. They should be encouraged to think of more qualities, animals, and other symbols. In addition, they can add a short saying or slogan. Many will look for "macho" or currently popular symbols of themselves. Attempt to get them to think more broadly than a mere imitation of someone else.

You might reinforce the idea for people to think both about themselves and as part of a team. Help individuals complete the five steps.

Once the team meetings begin, the goal is to establish a team identity. The five steps merely got them thinking about the issues so they would have something to contribute.

Although it is not required, anything that will allow students to add color to their coat of arms would be helpful. If nothing is available, students can finalize their projects at home.

Materials Required

Copies of the student materials should be made for all class members. In addition, extra copies of the blank coat of arms should be available.

Approximate Time

The classroom activities should last approximately 45 minutes to an hour, including the final discussion.

Discussion Questions

1. **Each team shall select someone to stand, display, and explain their coat of arms.**

   Hopefully, there will be a variety reflecting a wide range of qualities and concerns.

2. **Did you see a pattern in the kinds of qualities that were reflected in the coats of arms?**

   Students should realize that their age group, location, and shared experiences will tend to reflect the same qualities.

3. **Is there a difference between the contributions of girls and those of boys?**

   It will be interesting to see if anyone admits the differences.

4. **How many people had honesty, wisdom, or perseverance listed?**

   Hopefully, some of these qualities were mentioned.

5. **Which one did you like the best, and why?**

   This will reflect your class values.

6. **Can you think of other areas where symbols are used to signify someone's family, occupation, organization, or status?**

   This can include the following: a) sports teams, b) graduation robes, c) school or army uniforms, d) judges' robes, e) stripes or emblems showing military rank.

SUMMARY: Having a valuable purpose and pledging great qualities is usually a good method of bringing groups together. Some coats of arms may also include a slogan, such as "Semper Fidelis" or "Don't Tread on Me."

FOLLOW-UP: If students are interested in heraldry, you can assign them a project where they prepare an explanation of the various symbols used. In addition, this can be expanded to show a variety of forms of symbolic identification ranging from coats of arms and logos to uniforms.

HARDLY HERALDRY

Heraldry refers to a system of visual symbols used to identify the family backgrounds of noble Europeans. Although this kind of system started with primitive societies, we associate it with the medieval knights whose emblems or coats of arms provided a way for others to identify them at tournaments. In some ways, it is like a football jersey which identifies the team and the player.

Heraldry became a complicated subject because of centuries of traditions in which certain symbols had certain meanings. Animals are often associated with certain qualities that people would be proud to possess. The lion, eagle, and horse are common elements in the coats of arms and insignias in Great Britain, France, and Germany. In more primitive settings, tribes used actual parts of animals instead of graphic representations. Feathers, animal heads, sharks' teeth, and various animal skins have all been used by people to associate them with certain qualities that the bearer hoped to share.

Today, many organizations have ways of identifying themselves. They have developed a visual symbol which most people recognize and associate with a particular organization. Can you describe the symbol (trademark or logo) used by the following?

1. The National Broadcasting Company (NBC)
2. McDonalds
3. Chevrolet
4. The New York Yankees
5. The Marine Corps

You have been selected to serve on a team. This team will be asked to do certain things. Over a period of time, your team will take on an identity of its own. This identity will be shaped by its members and its purpose. It might be remembered for several years as one with imagination and an ability to get things done. The team might be seen by others as one whose members were proud to be associated with it. If you were to create your own coat of arms, what would it look like? How do you want to be viewed by others? What qualities do you hope to promote? What coat of arms would proudly represent you and your team? The United States Marine Corps has a saying "Semper Fidelis" which means "always faithful." If you added a saying to your coat of arms, what would it be?

GET STARTED

Each team is to create its own team coat of arms. You have been provided a blank shield upon which to add symbols. These symbols should represent the individuals and goals of your team. The following are some ideas to consider.

Step 1: Select from the list below three qualities that you think should represent your team.

Fair	Honest	Brave	Strong
Able to get it done	Smart	Wise	Funny
Experienced	Loyal	Winners	Respected
Helpful	Protective	Family-oriented	Shows initiative
Alert	Watchful	Tolerant	Beautiful

List your choices below.

a. ______________________________

b. ______________________________

c. ______________________________

Name ________________________________

Step 2: For choice *a*, select an animal which represents this quality. Write your choice of animal below.

____

Step 3: For choice *b* above, select a color which best represents this quality. Write your choice below.

____

Step 4: For choice *c*, select some other symbol to represent this quality. It might be a plant, object, or other familiar item. Write your choice below.

____

Step 5: Attempt to develop a short slogan or saying that will represent you or your team. Write it below.

____

Finally, meet as a team and review your choices in an attempt to create a team coat of arms. Your choice should represent the individuals that are members as well as your team's goals. At this point, your goals may only be to be constructive, original, and helpful. Discuss this and discuss the symbols and colors that should make up your team coat of arms. Complete this assignment by actually preparing a coat of arms. This will be the logo, trademark, or symbol that will represent you and your team. Make it something of which to be proud.

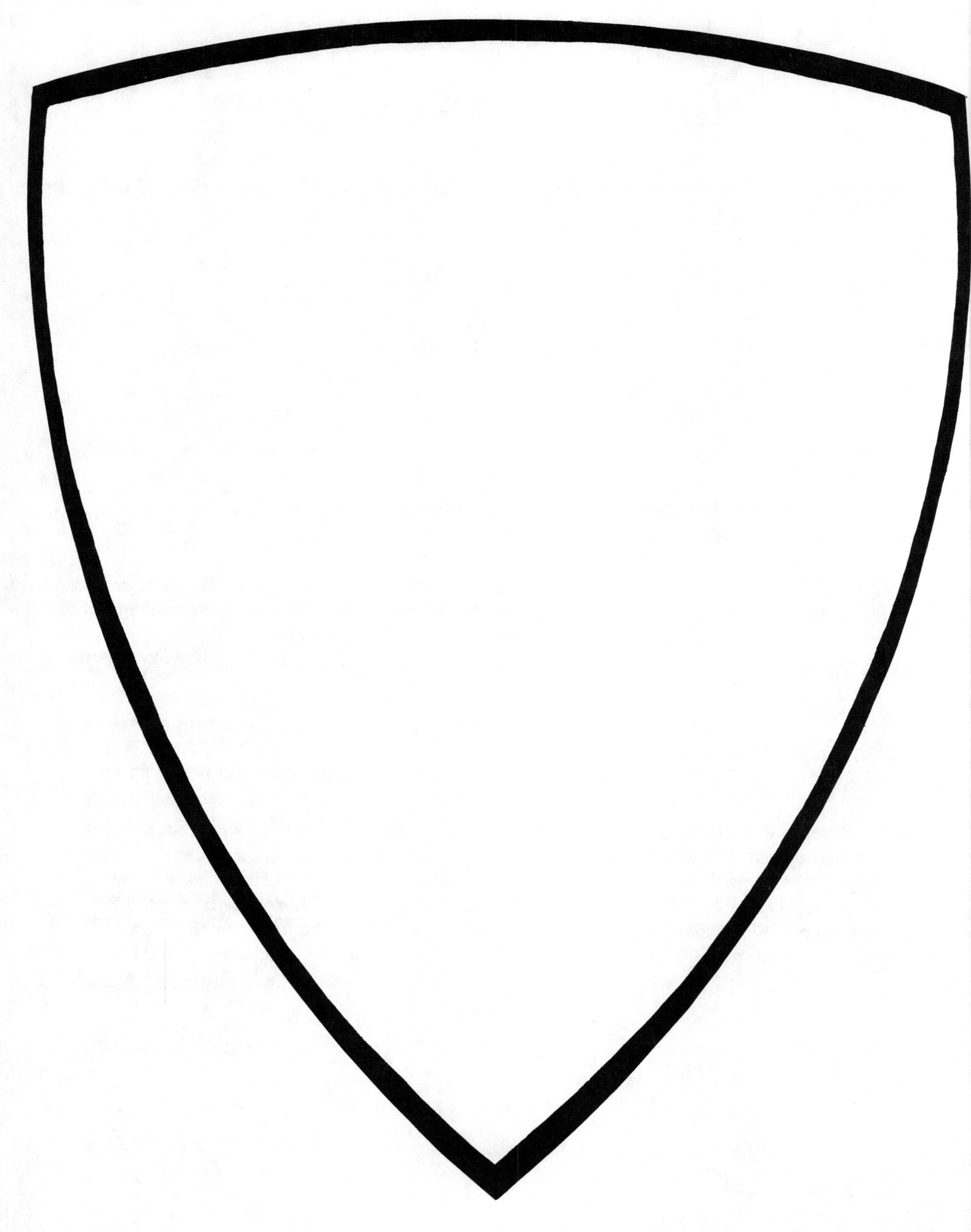

WHAT'S YOUR PROBLEM?

Objectives

- To illustrate methods of defining a problem so that the team can be focused in the proper direction and have methods for dealing with it. Remove yourself from the rut that caused the problem.
- To provide the teams with tools for considering problem statements prior to trying to solve the problem.

Procedure

Distribute copies of the reading assignment to all members of the class. DO NOT DISTRIBUTE THE PAGE CALLED "TEAM PROBLEM ASSESSMENTS" YET. Instruct them to take the next 10 minutes to read the materials. When all have completed the reading, ask them to move into the same teams as the ones in which they designed a coat of arms.

Instruct the teams that you will assign them one of the problem statements written on the next handout called "Team Problem Assessments." They should consider their problem and

1. Define the problem as one of the following: (A) **Why Technique;** (B) **Subdivide;** (C) **Specific;** or (D) **Verb Change**
2. Develop a restatement of the problem that more clearly defines the real problem.
3. Select a team member to present your results.

The team meeting should last about 15 minutes or until the team has completed its assignment.

What to Expect

The readings illustrate four methods of restating problems. If some students have difficulties with the concepts, you might think of other examples to help illustrate the points. You may find that some groups find this an easy task while others may have more difficulty.

Materials Required

Copy student materials and distribute to the class. Only one copy of the "Team Problem Assessment" is required for each team.

Approximate Time

The reading should last about 10 minutes. The team meetings should last another 10 to 15 minutes. The team reports should last 5 to 10 minutes, while the final question period could last another 5 minutes. Total estimated time is 45 minutes.

Responses From the Teams

1. **How can we improve upon the playground facilities of the school so that they will be of greater service to the community?**
   Subdivide: *Both the playground facilities and the community can be broken into smaller parts to focus on areas of service. Examples are the park area, the playground equipment, the gym, and the classrooms. Also, how could these things be of service to the retired, young families, or young children? How might the merchants of the area take advantage of the school playground?*

2. **How can we build a better mousetrap?**
   Why: *The trail to good answers might come from* ***why*** *you want a better mousetrap. The first answer might be, "To kill mice more effectively." Asking why again yields a better problem statement . . . "How might I keep my environment free of mice?"*

3. **How can we fix up the school dance?**
   Specific: *It might be easier to decide what aspect of the dance needs fixing and focus upon it.*

4. **In what ways might we improve upon the bicycle?**
   Subdivide: You *can break down the bicycle issue into such categories as (a) mechanical propulsion; (b) safety; (c) appearance; (d) steering; (e) passenger; (f) storage; (g) security; and (h) comfort.*

5. **How can we better paint the walls?**
   Verb: *Change the verb paint to "color," "cover," etc. You can rephrase the question to "How can we make the walls more interesting?"*

Discussion Questions

1. How many have trouble with the "why" technique?

This is the most difficult of the techniques. It requires that the answer to a "WHY" question be rephrased as a question. For example, in the team problem, the question is WHY do you want to build a better mousetrap? The answer, to catch mice better. Now you turn this answer into a question. WHY do you want to catch mice more effectively? Answer, so that I will never come in contact with them. Now that you have reached this level, you might focus on ways to keep your environment free of mice. To do so, your thinking can be expanded beyond the world of mousetraps into the whole universe while looking for a solution.

THE BILLIONS OF REGIONS OF YOUR MIND

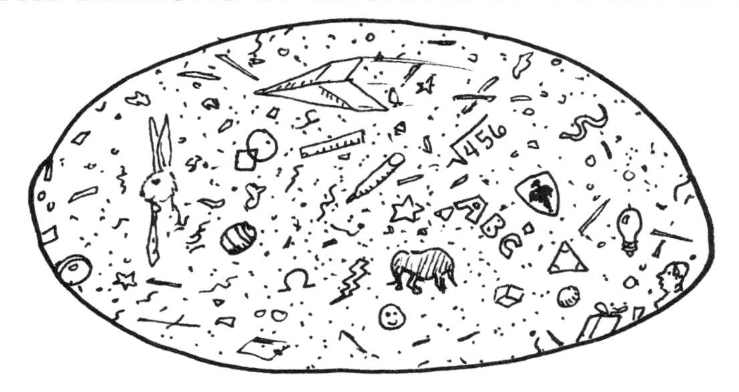

Mousetrap experience

2. Did the "Change verb" technique sound like a good idea? Did anyone think differently when you considered the word "store" instead of "park" cars?

This is really a technique to let your problem statement help to generate ideas by giving you a new mental picture of the problem. Remember, having the same mental picture to solutions that did not work in the past might only result in more solutions that do not work.

PARK **STORE**

WHAT'S YOUR PROBLEM?

Groups have spent hundreds of hours arguing about solutions to a perceived problem that was not actually the real problem. Can you imagine people arguing and fighting about something that was not even the problem? To illustrate, imagine the following situation:

The Board of Directors of the Alperstein Chemical Company have been arguing for days about the solution to their major problem. It seems that workers are quitting their jobs in the shipping department. To determine freight charges of the barrels of gunpowder shipped around the world, it is necessary to weigh the barrels. The present method is to have workmen lift the barrels onto scales, weigh them, and record the weight on a billing slip. Freight charges are determined by the number of miles to the destination times a dollar charge per pound of dynamite shipped.

For example, a barrel weighing 73.2 pounds being transported 500 miles at a per-pound cost of .09 would cost 500 x (73.2 pounds x $0.09) = $3294.00 to ship.

The problem being argued is how to keep workers who lift the barrels onto the scales from quitting. The arguments center on ways to keep the employees from quitting. One director wants to hire only big, strong men to lift the barrels onto the scales. Another wants to buy machines to lift the barrels.

The above problem can be compared to a person who has a terrible stomach ache. The big argument is whether the person should sit down or lie down. The real problem is what is causing the stomachache, whether it is serious, and what to do to eliminate the problem.

It is important to properly present a problem. You and your team do not want to waste your time working on symptoms. You want to solve problems. Presenting the problem correctly can do the following:

1. Make sure that we are pointed in the right direction.
2. Help us to generate ideas.
3. Prevent us from staying in the same rut that created the problem.

There are several techniques that a person or team can use to ensure that it is working on the real problem. The first we will call "The Why Technique."

THE WHY TECHNIQUE

In many cases a "fuzzy" situation appears as a problem which can be approached simply by asking "why"? Use the example mentioned earlier.

1. **WHY did men have to lift barrels onto the scales?** The answer was to weigh them.

2. **WHY did they weigh them?** The answer was so that freight charges could be determined. In the example, there was a charge of $.09 per pound times the number of miles travelled.

The new problem can be stated as **"In what ways might we determine freight charges for the gunpowder?"** With this problem statement you might focus on the real problem. With it, you might discover that gun powder can be manufactured in consistent weights so that it is not necessary to weigh anything. If you know what a cubic foot weighs, you can calculate the weight of any size shipment. This is a better approach than deciding how to keep workers from quitting their jobs.

THE SUBDIVIDING TECHNIQUE

Sometimes problems appear so big that you simply do not know where to begin. Consider the following problems:

1. How can we improve the school library?
2. How can world peace be accomplished?
3. How can I always feel good?
4. How might we "eat the elephant"?

Subdividing a problem into smaller parts makes it possible to focus on the parts more clearly. If your problem is to improve your school, you could break the problem into parts. The following might be smaller versions of the same problem:

1. How might we make learning more interesting?
2. How might school meals be more nutritious?
3. How might attendance be improved?
4. How might the school be used by the community when classes are not in session?

These are just four of many possibilities. If improvements can be made in any of the parts, there is improvement in the whole. The way to eat the elephant is "one bite at a time."

BE SPECIFIC

In some cases, it is important not to limit our thinking about the problem and its solutions. The "WHY" technique is good in this situation. For some problems, exactly the opposite is required. In the problem "How can I fix the car?" the possibilities seem immense. The problem might be more easily solved if we were to focus on what needs fixing. For example, "How can I get the car to start?"

This is similar to how a doctor works. If a doctor needs to treat a serious cut, he/she does not take chest X-rays or do a brain scan. The doctor needs to focus only on the problem.

CHANGE THE VERB

There are cases where the problem is clear but you need something to help in developing new solutions. The way the problem is phrased might help. Assume that the problem involves a lack of parking spaces in the city. In considering solutions, engineers phrased the problem as, "In what ways might we better park cars?" See what visions come into your mind as you consider the following problem statements where the verb has been changed:

1. How might we better store cars?
2. How might we better conceal cars?
3. How might we better package cars for storage?

TEAM MEETING

A short meeting of your team will take place after discussion of this reading. Your team will be presented a problem. You will be asked to apply one or more of these problem definition techniques as a way to prepare for solving it.

Name ______________________________

TEAM PROBLEM ASSESSMENTS

You will be asked to consider one of the problem statements listed below. As a team, you are to classify it into one of the four categories described in your reading. You are to agree on a restatement of the problem. This may be more than one statement. Select someone from your team to report to the group.

1. How can we improve upon the playground facilities of the school so that they will be of greater service to the community?

2. How can we build a better mousetrap?

3. How can we fix up the school dance?

4. In what ways might we improve the bicycle?

5. How can we better paint the walls?

____
____
____
____
____
____
____
____
____
____
____
____
____
____
____

JUST THE FACTS, MA'AM

Objective

To introduce the process of "fact finding" to team problem solving. This applies both to the introduction to the problem and potential solutions as well as testing various solutions against specific criteria.

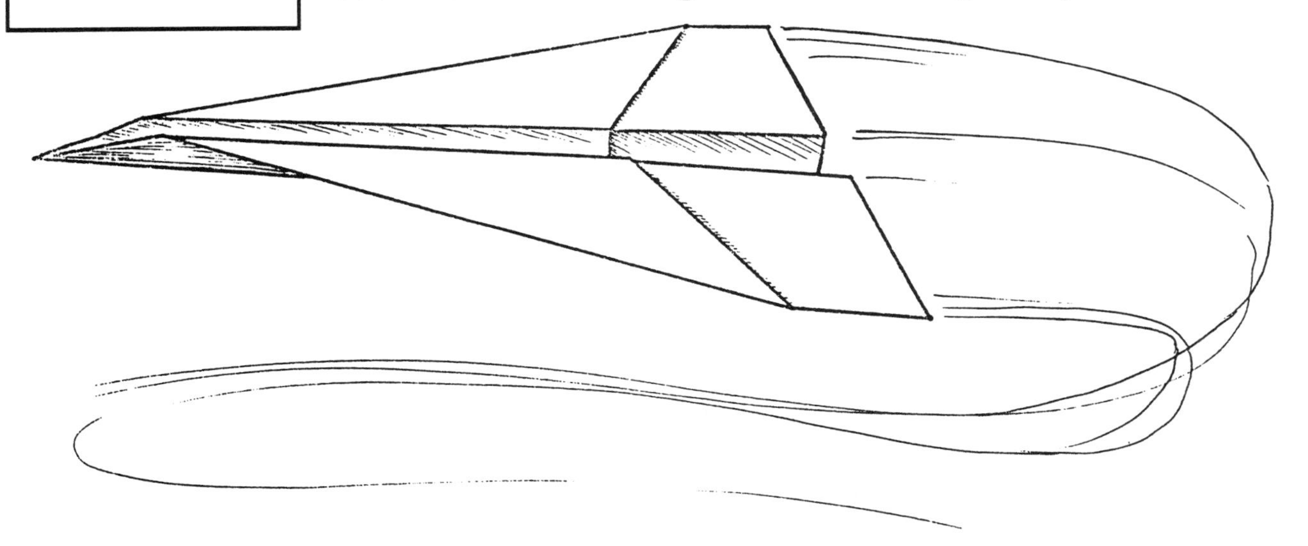

Procedure

Distribute copies of the student reading (first four pages). This describes the process of collecting data to test ideas. Upon completion of the reading, review the team problem to design a paper airplane of only the material which you provide each team. (This can be regular copy paper.)

Select a date and time approximately 7 to 10 days in the future for a competition between teams. At this time, each team will select the best airplane design for the competition. Prior to the first team meeting to plan strategy, distribute copies of the "Flight Tests." Explain that students are to:

1. Construct a paper airplane by folding the paper into shapes that will allow it to remain in flight for the maximum amount of time.

2. Conduct five test flights of the first design. Time each flight and record the time under the "Duration" column on the "Data Tables." Describe the method of launching the plane. Make sure that all tests are launched in exactly the same way so that modifications can be evaluated fairly.

3. Make three modifications to the original design and conduct three series of tests for each modification. Describe the modification that was made on the "Data Tables."

In the actual competition, each team will test its airplane three times. Each flight is timed. The score is the average flying time of the three flights. It is important that you and the teams establish a fair method of starting or propelling each plane into flight so that they all begin flight in exactly the same manner. This might be simply pushing each off a ledge.

The actual purpose of the activity is to:

1. Allow teams to collect information about a problem. In this case, some team member should be assigned to check the library for any sources of information about paper airplanes. It may be that there are books on the subject which describe good design ideas.

2. Collect data on test flights as a tool to analyze problems and make improvements. In the example of the catapult, a form of "Scatter Diagram" is used showing exact test results. This form of data collection tends to show patterns of problems. In the airplane problem, flying times are recorded and modifications are noted. This is a graphic method of displaying cause and effect.

3. Provide an interesting problem for teams to resolve.

Prior to the competition, teams must hand in their "Data Tables for Flight Tests." After the competition, a representative can explain the team's testing procedures to the class. In particular, he/she should explain anything discovered that improved the performance of their paper airplane.

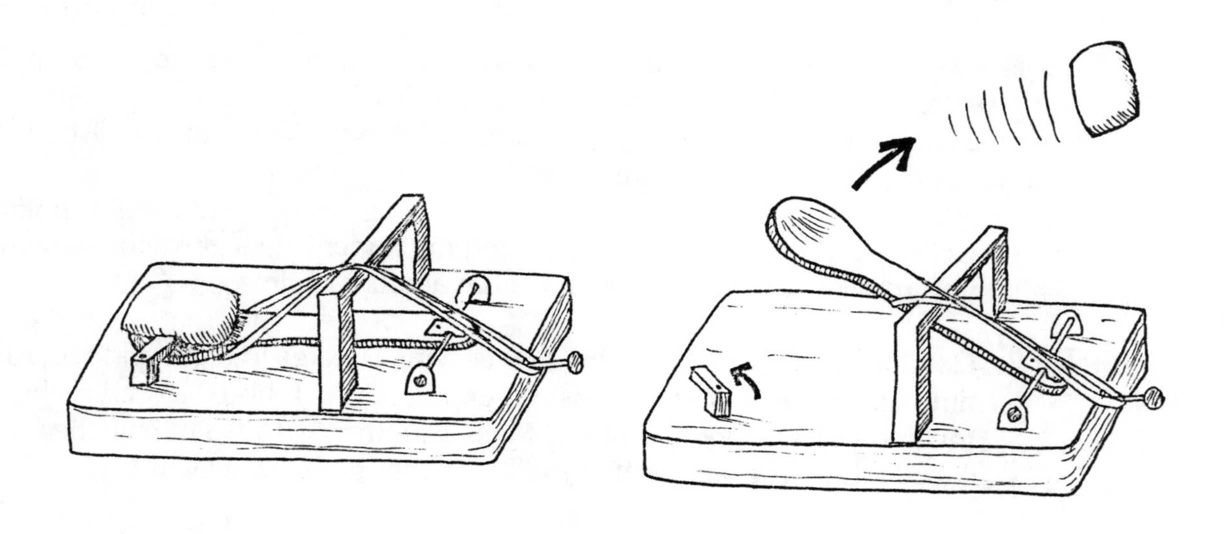

What to Expect

Many students will want to rush into the project by folding and launching airplanes. Some might prefer to work on the catapult problem. (You be the judge.) Keep them focused on the idea of seeing if there is any information about paper airplanes. After all, why reinvent the wheel? Encourage teams to call their own meetings and to plan tests on their own. Hopefully, you will see some team camaraderie begin to develop.

Materials Required

In addition to the handouts, sheets of blank paper should be distributed to each team for use as paper airplanes.

Approximate Time

The approximate time of the reading is 15 minutes. Discussions might last another 15 minutes. A short team meeting should be held so that each can plan its strategy for the flying competition. This should not last over 15 minutes.

Note that you might either set aside times for meetings and tests over the next several days or require that teams meet on their own time.

You must select a time for the competition. The ideal place would be an empty gym, the cafeteria, or the parking lot. The competition will take approximately 30 minutes.

Discussion Questions

1. **What was the most difficult part of this activity?**

   This answer will vary from group to group. Hopefully, it was not that the team dynamics broke down.

2. **Did anyone find information about paper airplanes that helped in this project?**

   Hopefully, some teams found information that helped in this project. One of the points of this activity was to gather information about the problem. It is better to start solving a problem with the knowledge provided by others than to start from "square one."

3. **Did anyone learn anything from keeping the flight control data?**

   Again, this answer will vary from group to group. Some will feel that it only slowed them down while others will see it as a useful tool.

4. **Will a member of each team describe their modifications and test results with the class?**

   Each team should select a spokesperson to describe the team's efforts in the competition.

JUST THE FACTS, MA'AM

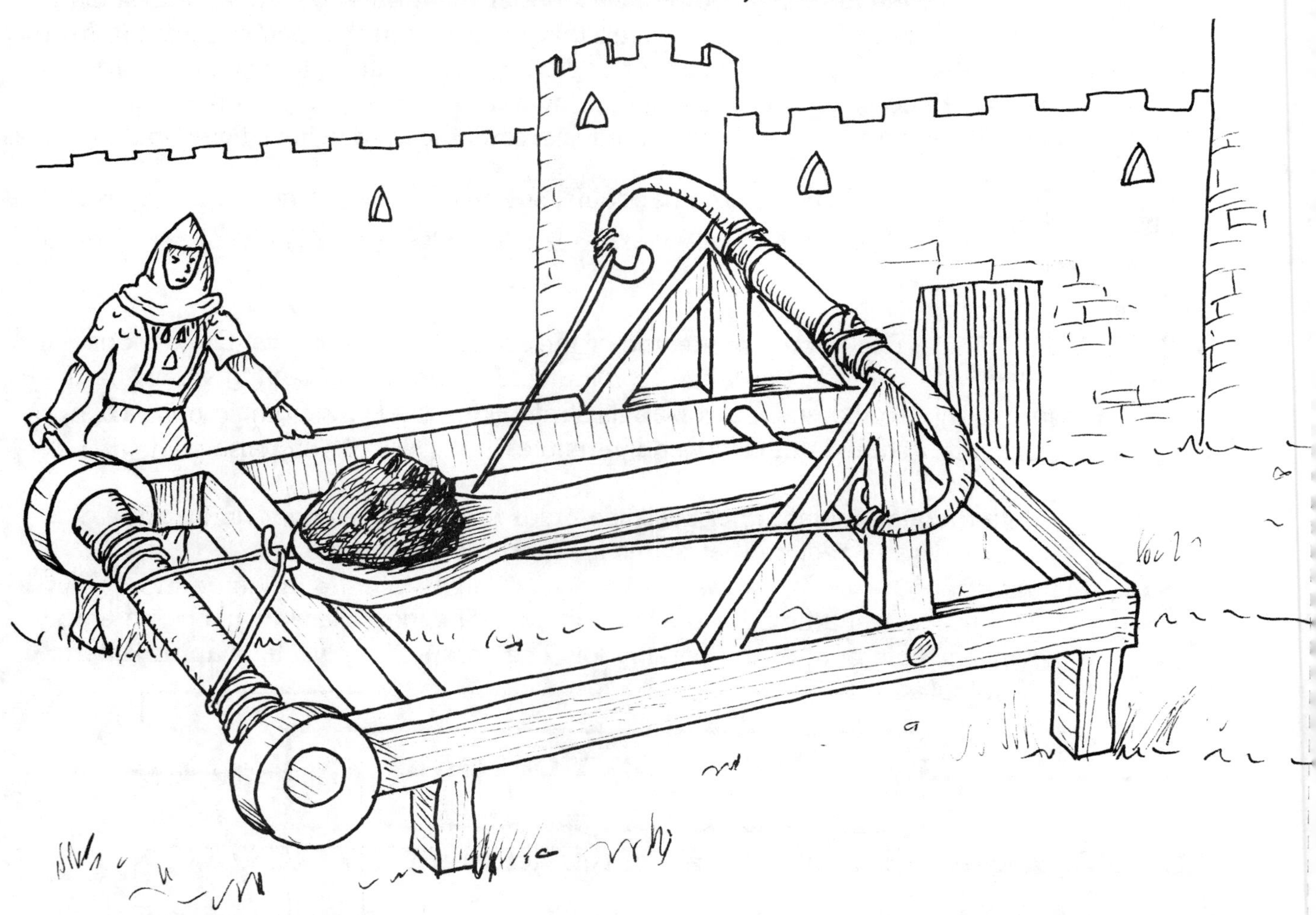

When attempting to solve a problem you need accurate information. You cannot base an important decision on rumors or guesses. In developing your problem statement and approaches to solutions, it is necessary to set aside time to study the issues and gather information. In problem solving, this is called "The Fact Finding Stage."

Imagine considering three alternative solutions to the problem of preventing your dog from running away. Each of the three ideas has a great deal of support. You decide to test each plan and produce the following test results:

PLAN	# TESTS	# TIMES DOG RAN AWAY
1.	10	4
2.	10	2
3.	10	0

There is no longer any point in arguing about plans #1 and #2. They do not work. Only plan #3 had the desired results.

When a team is developing solutions to problems, they must schedule time to gather information about the problem and time to test their ideas to make sure their solution achieves the desired results. To illustrate in greater detail, assume that your team was given the following assignment:

Your team is to develop a *catapult.* This is an ancient military device which projected missiles through the air. Yours must meet the following specifications:

1. It must be constructed at home using common materials found in a hardware store for less than $1.00.

2. It must be stationary, that is, it cannot be hand-held.

3. The only human assistance that may be given is in placing the projectile onto the catapult, cocking it, and releasing a triggering mechanism. It must otherwise stand alone.

4. It must throw a bean bag (projectile) into a 2' x 2' square 90 percent of the time.

5. Its minimum range shall be no less than 8 feet and its maximum range no more than 11 feet.

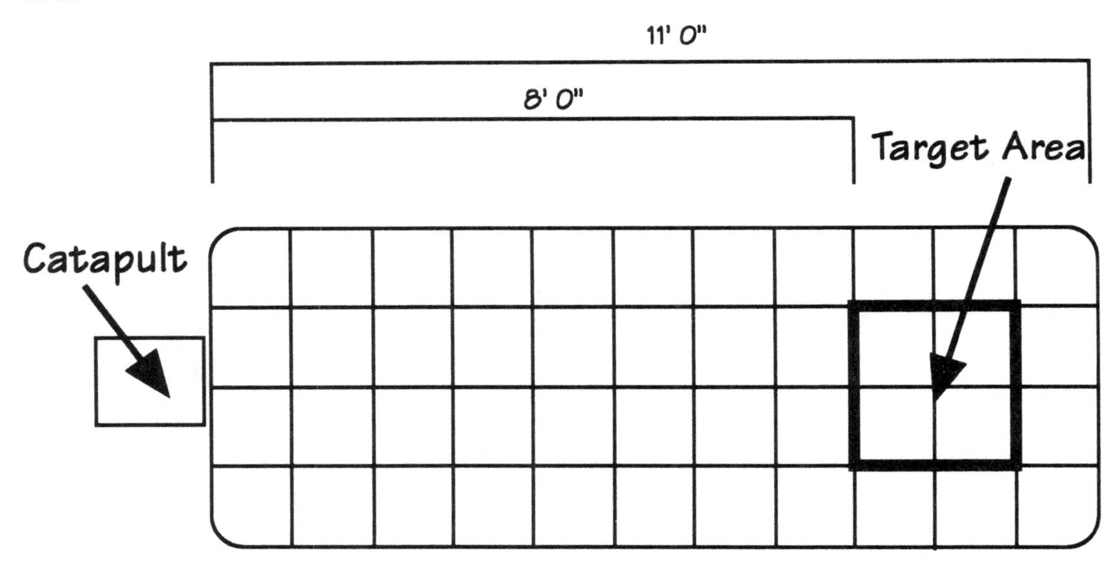

Your first fact-finding problem may be to learn what materials would be appropriate to use. Pieces of wood, rubber bands, and other materials are suggested by your team. Team members finally develop a design and construct the catapult.

Next, you must test your device to see if it meets the requirements. During the process of testing, use charts similar to those shown below to illustrate the results of your tests. You continue to modify your catapult until it meets specifications (9 out of 10 shots landing inside the target area). (See Test #1.)

Test #1
Location of landing-10 times

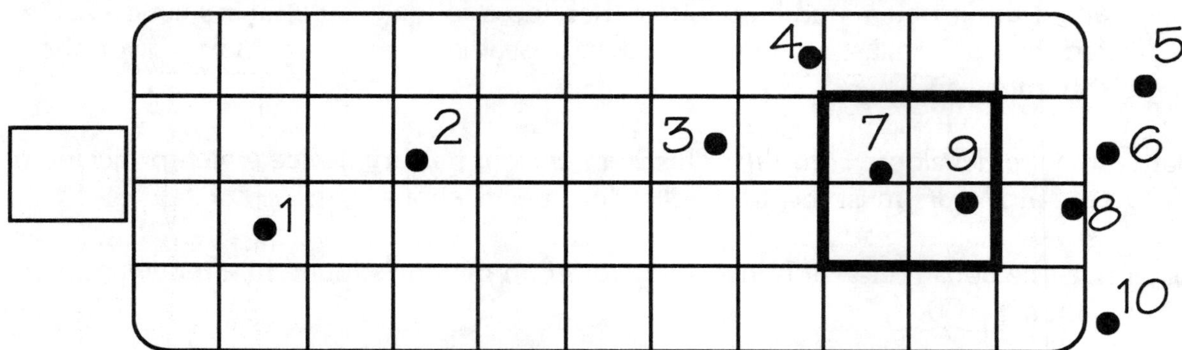

This information about your first test illustrates the results. If each had been numbered, you could begin to understand what your problems were. In this case there is too great a variation between shots. You might decide to use two rubber bands instead of one. Test this idea. (See Test #2.)

Test #2

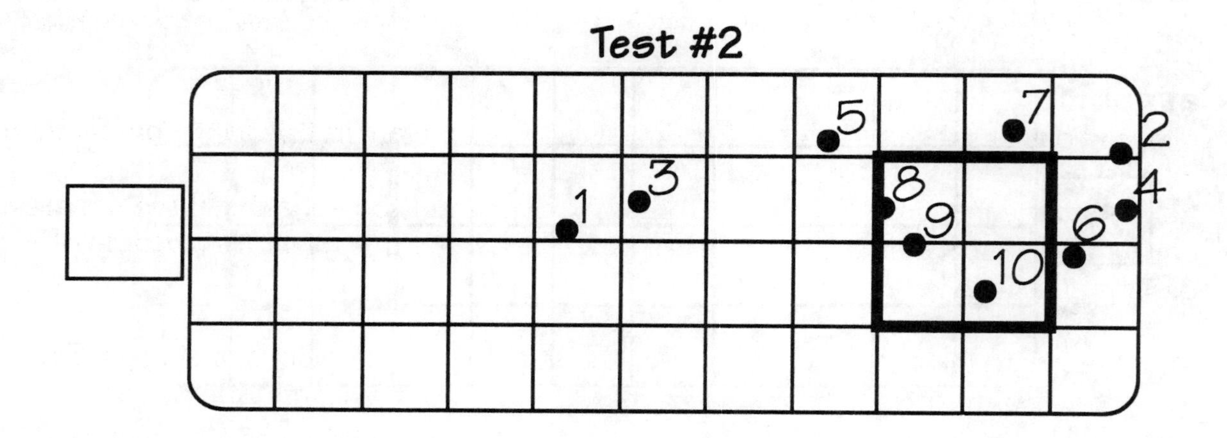

Your adjustments reduced the range or variation of the scattered shots. A team member observes that the catapult platform slipped on all of the shots that landed short of the target. Your next adjustment is to add something heavy to the platform so that it will not move when it is fired. (For the results, see Test #3.)

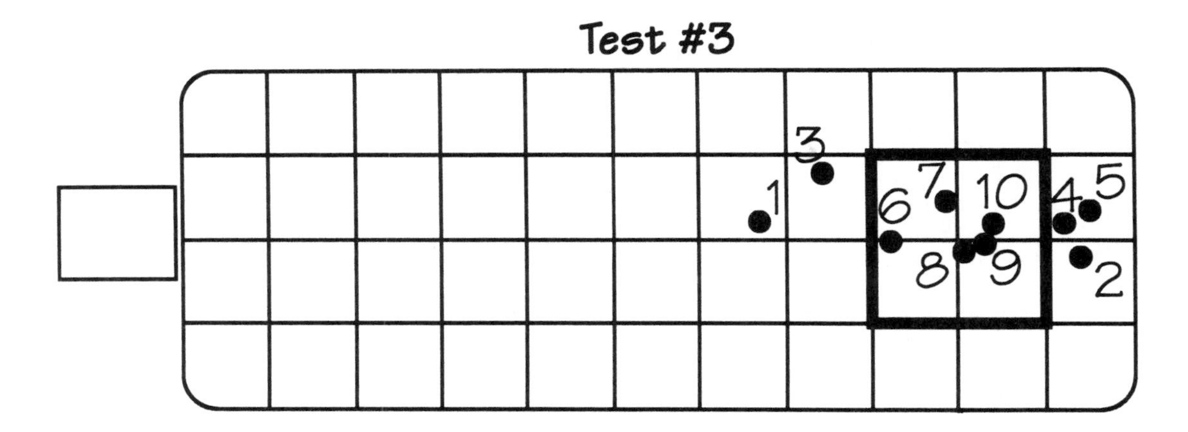

Whatever changes were made improved the performance of the catapult. The spread or variation is narrower. You would continue to make modifications until you reached your goal.

To follow up on the approach of data collection, your team will compete with other classroom teams on a project. You are to design an airplane constructed of paper provided by your teacher. You may fold, cut, or add other materials to the paper in developing a design that will solve the problem.

The following outlines the procedures to be followed by your team in the flying competition:

1. You are to meet and assign responsibilities. For example, someone might see if there is any written information about paper airplanes. Someone else might try a variety of designs and see how they work.

2. Your team is to test a minimum of four different plane configurations or shapes. Each test consists of five flights. You are to maintain a chart of the length of time each remained in the air before it first touched the ground. You must make sure that in each trial the plane was launched in exactly the same way. Upon the completion of the competition, you are to hand in your data test results. They should include notes about the changes made in each series of tests.

3. In the final competition, each team will launch its plane in exactly the same manner. The one remaining in the air the longest wins.

Name ______________________________

DATA TABLES FOR
FLIGHT TESTS

TEST #1

DURATION	DESCRIPTION OF LAUNCHING PROCEDURE
1. ______	______
2. ______	______
3. ______	______
4. ______	______
5. ______	______

TEST #2

DURATION	DESCRIPTION OF MODIFICATION
1. ______	______
2. ______	______
3. ______	______
4. ______	______
5. ______	______

TEST #3

DURATION	DESCRIPTION OF MODIFICATION
1. ______	______
2. ______	______
3. ______	______
4. ______	______
5. ______	______

TEST #4

DURATION	DESCRIPTION OF MODIFICATION
1. ______	______
2. ______	______
3. ______	______
4. ______	______
5. ______	______

ANIMAL, VEGETABLE, OR FRENCH FRY?

Objective

To understand the importance of asking good questions in problem-solving situations. Using a common group game, practice the ability to ask questions which eliminate a great number of possibilities as a way of quickly focusing upon the problem.

Procedure

Ask class members to read the two-page activity (pp. 84-85) and to evaluate the nine questions on the second page. When this is complete, discuss the nine questions (see Discussion Questions).

After a discussion of the questions, you might try a few rounds of the game. Do so with the idea that the class is to see whether the percentage of good questions being asked has increased.

What to Expect

This is a pleasant activity which can generate a lot of enthusiasm. You will find that some people will have trouble developing a good question at first. Only after some experience with a game like this do students become more comfortable.

Materials Required

Only copies of the student materials are required.

Approximate Time

The readings and discussions will last only 20 to 30 minutes. If you choose to play several rounds with the class, it will last another 30 minutes.

Discussion Questions

(After reading)

1. How did you evaluate the questions from the second page of the activity?

a. The first question is a great one since it narrows the range of possibilities by as many as two-thirds. If the answer is "yes," you have eliminated things. If the answer is no, you have eliminated people and places. This really cuts down the choices.

b. Obviously this is a poor first question since it eliminates only one out of billions of possibilities.

c. This is a fair question. It determines whether or not your idea is something that is man-made.

d. Now that you know it is a place, it could be anywhere in the solar system. This question is bad because it eliminates only one of them.

e. Asking if the location is in North America eliminates a large section of the globe. This is a good question.

f. This is also a good question. It eliminates all of the places that would not be considered as vacation destinations.

g. This is a weak question. Knowing that it is a vacation destination in the United States, you wasted a question by focusing on only a small area of the country.

h. This is a good question. It narrows the possibilities to the western states.

i. This is a good question in this position. It is similar to question #3 which was not appropriate then. You have now eliminated either natural locations (i.e., Yosemite, Pike's Peak, Grand Canyon) or man-made vacation areas such as Disneyland, Knott's Berry Farm, or Marineland.

2. If you were to tell others how you must think to develop good questions, what would you tell them?

This is valuable for the people who find this difficult. Some students might say that you have to think in categories. You have to see whole categories (i.e., animal, vegetable, other) and keep subdividing until your last category is small enough for you to make a reasonable guess.

To illustrate, if you were to know that someone is thinking of a person, some of the categories would be: a.) living or dead, b.) man or woman, c.) occupation, d.) if alive, general age, e.) if dead, time in which he/she lived.

3. If you were assigned to look for information about and designs for paper airplanes, where would you look?

Have students think categorically. Would you look in the kitchen, the gym, or the library? If the library, where would you look? Hopefully, students can see that the game skills applied to a variety of issues.

FOLLOW-UP: These kinds of thinking activities that are necessary in problem solving can be rehearsed in many ways. Another activity involves students trying to discover what certain objects are by asking questions about their physical properties. For example, an ice cube is concealed in something. Students must establish its identity by asking questions about its physical properties (i.e., Is it a liquid?).

ANIMAL, VEGETABLE, OR FRENCH FRY?

Being able to ask good questions is a skill that can be learned. It is also a skill critical in any form of problem solving. Being able to ask questions which lead us in the right direction gets to where we want to go a lot faster than asking "dumb" questions.

Investigations, whether you are a doctor or a detective, often involve a process of eliminating possibilities. Good questions eliminate a lot of possibilities. Bad questions eliminate only one.

One method of practicing this skill is in the game known under several names which include "20 Questions," "Animal, Vegetable, or Mineral," or "Person, Place, or Thing." This is how the game is played:

1. You are in a group and are the first to start. You must think of something and not tell anyone what it is. You might write it down before starting, but keep it a secret until the end. You think of a person, place, or thing. It could be classified as animal, vegetable, or mineral. Let's say that you think of "The Grand Canyon."

Name ___________________________

2. The others in the group must ask you questions (in turn) which can be answered only with a yes or no response.

3. Since they are allowed only 20 questions, it is important that the questions be ones which eliminate as many possibilities as possible so that the choices become fewer. (Now you can see that if someone asked if you were thinking of a French fry they would eliminate only one choice in billions of possibilities.)

4. The game is over when someone correctly identifies what you were thinking or after the twentieth question.

Assume that you are now playing the game and the following are questions that are being addressed to you. Evaluate them by placing a check mark in the appropriate column.

	Good	Bad	Question
a.	_______	_______	Are you thinking of something that is either a person or a place?
b.	_______	_______	Are you thinking of a peanut butter sandwich?
c.	_______	_______	Is this something that is manufactured?

Assume that the group knows you are thinking of a place. Evaluate the following questions:

	Good	Bad	Question
d.	_______	_______	Are you thinking of East Cicero, Illinois?
e.	_______	_______	Is the place in North America?
f.	_______	_______	Is this place a vacation destination?

Assume that the group knows the place is in the United States and that it is a tourist destination. Evaluate these questions.

	Good	Bad	Question
g.	_______	_______	Can we walk to this place from here in one day?
h.	_______	_______	Is it located in the western states?
i.	_______	_______	Is it natural as opposed to man-made?

STRATEGIC THINKING

Objective

To introduce, learn, and apply strategic thinking as a problem-solving tool. Teams select interesting problems on which to apply this strategy.

Procedure

As a class, ask students to read the three-page assignment. During the reading, individuals are to write 10 things that would be true (or likely) if they were still attending this school after starring in a hit TV series. After they have written their comments, you can stop the reading and ask what some of them wrote.

Have the class resume the reading, which uses as an example a school newspaper. It gives examples of what would be seen if there was a school paper.

Either during this class session or the next one, divide the class into their assigned teams and

1. Have them select one of the 10 topics listed.

2. As a group, have them record 12 things that they would see if their project (topic) were completed magnificently.

What to Expect

Some students may want clarification of what is meant by describing what you would see if the problem were solved. Hopefully, your examples and those provided by others will help them to understand the process.

Students will enjoy the first task of describing what life would be like if they were the star of a hit TV series. This will be fun for them to report. When they report on their selected topic, look for increasing depth in their observations. It is a good sign to see them progress from basic to more in-depth understanding, with observations that range from obvious to subtle.

Materials Required

Only copies of the reading are necessary. It would be helpful for teams to have a "flipchart" to record team observations.

Approximate Time

This could be two class sessions of approximately 45 minutes each. If you spend a good deal of time in discussions of the TV star and school newspaper topics, the team assignment should take place on the next session of Team Problem Solving.

Discussion Questions

(After reading)

1. What would you see if you were a cast member of a hit TV show?

Each student can be sure that many more of his/her classmates would want to be a friend, while others would be jealous. There would be many interruptions for TV assignments, photographers, and interviews. Students probably would not have time for many of their school activities. They may even have to enroll in a private school where they are tutored, instead of attending classes.

2. Regarding the school newspaper example, assume that the school could not participate in any way but the paper developed just as described in your reading:

a. How many students are involved and what do they do?

There had to be a lot of students involved who did everything from decide what the paper was about, to getting support from the community, writing articles, laying out material, taking pictures, getting the paper printed and distributed.

b. Where is the office for the paper?

The office must be in someone's home or perhaps space is available in some store in town. Where might someone lend the space where materials would be safe and students would have access before school and/or after school?

c. Where did you get your supplies and equipment?

It may have been possible for local merchants to donate older equipment, particularly if they saw the project as valuable.

d. Why would the students pay to receive your newspaper?

The only reason anyone would pay for something is if it was good. If it is well done, interesting, and consistently of high quality, everyone will cooperate with the project. If it is poorly done and meant only to amuse some people, the class would not get cooperation from the community, school, or even some of the students.

e. Why would the school allow you to sell the paper in the school?

Because it is such a good paper. It is well written and a worthy project. The school will even be able to take credit for being smart enough to let the students do it.

f. Considering the staff of the newspaper as a big team, what roles (jobs or responsibilities) must have been in place for this project to be such a success?

There is need for a strong leadership role. Someone must be the boss who decides what and what not to print. A school newspaper can easily become a cheap, sloppy way of being funny, and someone has to have the "guts" to say no and maintain high standards. This is always the responsibility of the editor-in-chief.

There have to be people who can write interesting things in interesting ways. These are the reporters.

Students should identify other roles such as those who were able to sell advertising and the idea of a paper to get others to contribute to the project.

Allow students to recommend other roles.

g. Why would the community merchants support the newspaper?

Because it is a responsible activity conducted by responsible people. It can even benefit the merchants by advertising to the student market or others who buy their products.

3. **After the teams have worked up their topic, have each report how they set up their problem.**

   Each team should read their list of 12 things.

4. **When developing assumptions based upon a fact (or assumed fact), we will see ideas that appear as obvious while others will seem subtle.**

   Example: little green men . . . flying saucer

   Obvious: There is another life form capable of spaceflight.

   Subtle: Air traffic is curtailed at Baltimore and Dulles airports in the belief that there is a national emergency.

STRATEGIC THINKING

In his book *The World of Robert Heinlein,* the author claimed that he would start a project by asking "What if?" What if little green men landed on the White House lawn? This famous science fiction writer used a process which some call strategic thinking. This is a great problem-solving tool because it allows you to visualize what things would be like if your problem were solved.

You may think that this requires a great deal of imagination. With practice, you can become very good at developing the details after viewing the big picture.

Think about the "little green men" situation. What do you think would happen if little green men were to land their flying saucer on the White House lawn? Your team could spend all day developing ideas. How would the army react? What would the press do? Why are they here? Are they friend or foe?

This is an interesting way to develop ideas about a story. The same skill is also used in solving many problems. If you can visualize what happens when the problem is solved, you can outline in great detail all of the things that have to be done to arrive at your solution. Try an example.

If you were asked tomorrow to star in an episode of a hit TV show, what would things be like for you in school after it was seen by everyone in town?

Think of 10 things and write them down on the next page.

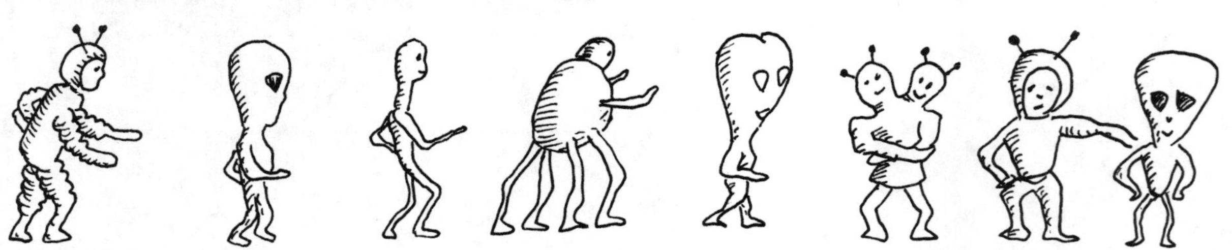

Name ________________________________

NOW THAT EVERYONE IN TOWN SAW THE TV SHOW, HOW WOULD THINGS BE DIFFERENT IN SCHOOL? (WITH YOUR FRIENDS)

1. ____

____

2. ____

____

3. ____

____

(WITH YOUR TEACHERS?)

4. ____

____

5. ____

____

6. ____

____

(IF YOU WERE ASKED TO APPEAR IN ANOTHER EPISODE?)

7. ____

____

8. ____

____

(IF YOU WERE ASKED TO APPEAR AS A GUEST ON A LATE NIGHT TALK SHOW?)

9. ____

____

10. ____

____

Name ______________________________

The way this process works as a tool in problem solving is by describing what you will see once the problem is solved. Another way to look at it is by asking what you will not see as well.

Assume that your problem involves starting a school newspaper. You never had one and your school could not afford it if they had wanted one. How would you approach this problem? If you were to visualize what things looked like if your problem was solved, describe what you would see. For example:

1. A group of students are assigned various responsibilities for the production of the paper. There are reporters, editors, people who sell advertising, and some who take pictures.
2. You have the necessary funds for an operating budget.
3. On a regular basis, the school paper is distributed (monthly, every two weeks, etc.).
4. There is a newspaper office with files, work areas, and equipment.
5. Local advertisers pay the paper to circulate their ads in the newspaper. These include regular ads and coupons.
6. Nearly all of the work is done before and after school hours. Some of your teachers allow time from writing class to work on the paper.

You continue this process of describing what you would see as long as you can. On the problem above, complete the sentences as a way of focusing on the results.

1. The most popular feature in the paper is

____

____

2. Your readers will tell you that the least interesting section of the paper is

____

____

3. My favorite page is ______________________________
   because ______________________________

Name________________________________

4. The paper has been appreciated by the people living around the school because
____
____

5. The following is the favorite section of the paper for the following people:
(example: computer buffs—The computer program reviews)

Group	Section
a.__________	__________________
b.__________	__________________
c.__________	__________________
d.__________	__________________

6. The hardest job on the newspaper is
____
____

7. We have come close to getting in trouble because of __________
____
____

8. Our greatest cost in running the newspaper has been __________
We were able to cover this expense by__________________
____

What you have is a specific description of where you want to go. You know where you are now, you know exactly where you are going; all you have to do is decide how you are going to get there. Using this problem, you can imagine what problems your team will face and what roles will be required.

Now review what you have said, assume that you are there, and ask how you did it. In doing so, you will come up with answers like these:

1. Some teams went into the community and got support from local businesses. They found someone to help with space and advertising revenue. Some found businesses to donate typewriters and older computers.

2. Team members were able to select those whose talents were for writing, editing, and managing. They assembled a staff of dedicated people who were willing to give their own time to produce the paper.

3. Someone or a group was able to get support from the school for distributing the paper. The school may also have contributed in many other ways, but someone had to sell the idea.

As you continue to question how you got to your solution, you begin to organize your problem in terms of what you will have to do.

On the next page is listed a variety of problems. As a team, select one of them and go through this process by completing the questionnaire that you will receive.

TOPICS

1. As a team project, you want to start a school bookstore which is open 30 minutes before school, 30 minutes after school, and during the lunch hour. Profits from the sales go to your team treasury.

2. As a team project, you want to start a drama group in the school which produces its own plays and musicals. There is no stage facility in your school.

3. As a fund-raising project you want to set up a fruit juice stand in the school before classes in the morning.

4. You want your school science club to be the best in the United States.

5. You organize a baby-sitting service which includes a team of trained people and serves as a small company that makes money.

6. Your team invents classroom learning games that are used throughout the school system in your town.

7. A section of your school library is set aside for the works of student authors.

8. The school band stays together in the summers and plays concerts in the park.

9. Your team has produced taped recordings of events in American History that are available to people in retirement homes.

10. As a fund-raiser, your team has a store which sells used sporting goods.

Name ______________________________

HOW TO SET UP YOUR PROBLEM

Assume that your problem has been solved and is underway. List 12 things that you see or that must be true.

1. ______________________________
____
2. ______________________________
____
3. ______________________________
____
4. ______________________________
____
5. ______________________________
____
6. ______________________________
____
7. ______________________________
____
8. ______________________________
____
9. ______________________________
____
10. ______________________________
____
11. ______________________________
____
12. ______________________________
____

IT'S A TIE

Objective

To apply the various skills introduced in team problem solving to a specific issue. The problem is determining the rate at which people learn to tie a tie using written instructions. The teams are to devise improved methods for such learning and prove their methods to be more effective.

Procedure

Before assembling the class into teams, distribute the reading materials. You may wish to discuss the reading by sections. For this reason, the "question" section is divided into the topics of the student reading.

Explain that the "Meeting Agendas" are to be used by the teams as a recommended set of guidelines for the meetings used for planning, executing, and implementing their plan.

You should announce a time approximately 30 days in the future when the team assignments are to be completed. At this time, each team should present data comparing their idea for instructing people to tie ties against the method of simply providing written instructions. The data would show times required for a number of people to tie ties using two different learning techniques. In addition, each team should select a spokesperson to describe the steps taken by the team to complete their task.

All of the teams are going to have a logistics problem. Where do they find 10 people who do not know how to tie a tie, test them using only a set of printed instructions, and conduct a similar test using a method that they have created?

Although this problem is to be solved by each team, you might be able to help them. For example, you might suggest that 10 members of the class test the written instructions method and be timed. This data can be used as the "control" for all of the teams.

Cooperate with the teams in establishing ground rules for their three to five meetings required over the next 30 days. You may provide classroom time for them or insist that they be held during lunch hours or even on their own time. Once the schedule has been established by the teams, your role may be that of advisor.

What to Expect

This is an opportunity for some groups to take charge, define their plan, and act on it. Some will seize upon the opportunity; others will not. You will probably find that there were not enough "take charge" types to go around. Nevertheless, the more opportunities to take a leadership role, the more likely people will take the challenge.

Materials Required

In addition to copies of the reading (3 pages) for each student and the ballots, you will need copies of agendas and planners for each team. Each group will have to get 10 ties to conduct their tests.

Approximate Time

The initial class session will require approximately 45 minutes including the first team meeting. Other team meetings will be required over the next 30 days. The final presentation should last 30 minutes.

Discussion Questions

"CLEAR PURPOSE"

1. What is your assignment?

If your team has been successful, what will you have done? Everyone must understand that they will have considered many ways to instruct someone on how to tie a tie. A promising idea was selected and tested. This test clearly established that this method was more effective than another method because it took people less time to tie the tie correctly.

"A PLAN"

2. What is meant by "a plan"?

The team is to plan and implement everything from writing instructions on how to tie a tie (for the initial "control" tests) to assigning people responsibilities, conducting meetings, checking progress, making or creating whatever is needed, and conducting a second set of tests. Finally, the plan must include preparing a comparison of data (test results) showing this plan to be superior.

The class must be able to clarify that each team is to make a plan and make the plan happen.

"CLEAR ROLES"

3. The reading refers to "Clear Roles." What does this mean?

Earlier activities ("Mission Impossible") attempted to point out that to accomplish something with a team requires that people play different roles. Some can develop good ideas, others can make things, while others can contribute in other ways. The issue of developing tests and ideas and implementing a plan will require that different people do different things. People's roles may not always suit them or be what they want them to be. Nevertheless, there are jobs to be done and someone has to do them.

Some students might find it difficult to ask others to do something. This is part of leadership; someone usually takes charge and needs the help of others. Hopefully, everyone can rehearse this role.

"GROUND RULES"

4. Why is the idea of "Ground Rules" an important part of successful team operations?

Students should express that for things to get done, everyone has to respect the procedures and one another. They should listen, express their opinions, vote for what they believe is the best idea, and then support the decisions of the group. Sometimes their views will be observed, sometimes they will not.

IT'S A TIE

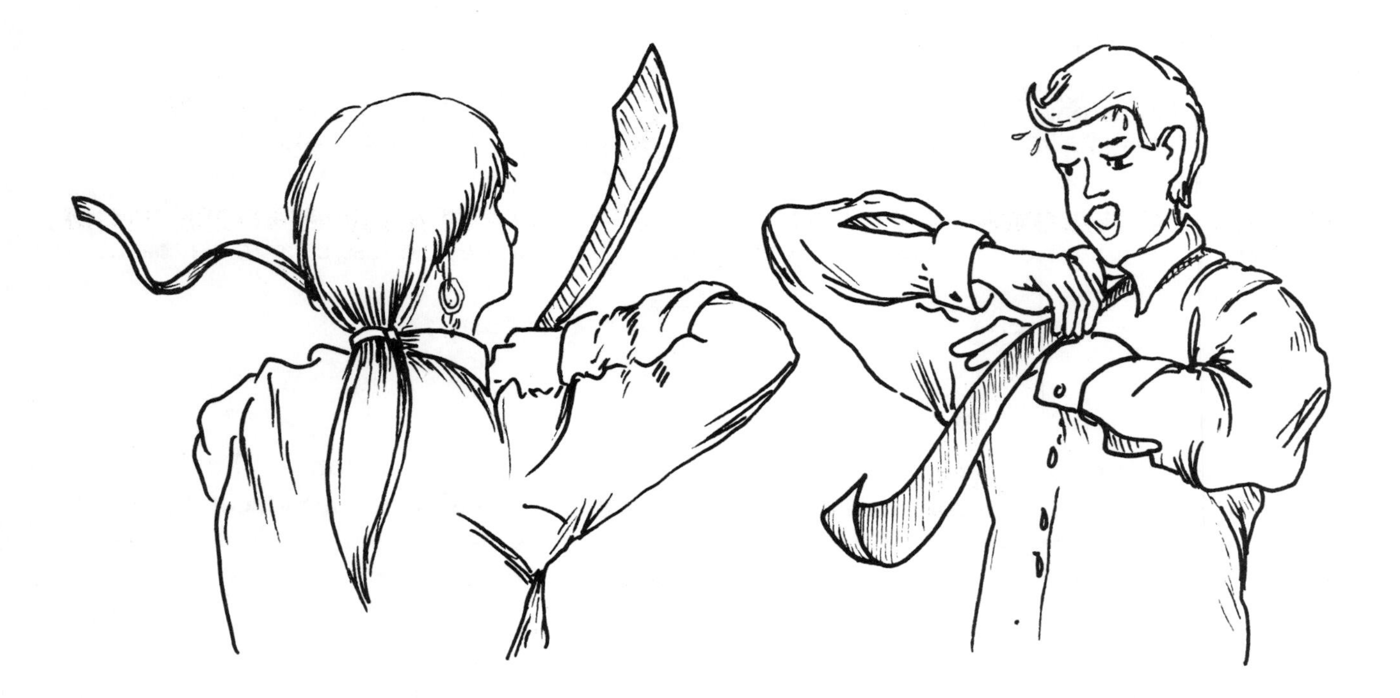

How many in the room know how to tie a tie? Do you know how hard it is to teach someone who does not know how to tie one? It is tough. This fact presents a great opportunity for your team to apply all that it has learned and also to benefit mankind. Your team is to develop a system to teach others to tie a tie. To reinforce effective team dynamics, you will go through the various elements that have been presented throughout these activities.

A CLEAR PURPOSE

As a team, your goals are these:

1. Develop an improved method of teaching people to tie ties.

2. Determine how long it takes for someone who does not know how to tie a tie, given only verbal instructions.

3. Develop and test methods for instructing someone else to tie a tie. Determine the method that is the most effective (the method which requires someone the least amount of time using your technique).

4. Be able to prove that your method produces better results than simply having someone who knows explaining to someone who does not know how to tie a tie.

5. Your project has been successfully completed when you can show data proving that people can tie their ties faster using your teaching technique than with another method.

6. Complete the project within 30 days.

To explain, "show data" refers to your main test results in a way that "speaks for itself." Review the following test results and see if you could explain their conclusions.

NUMBER OF THROWS OUT OF 10 TO PASS THROUGH AN INNERTUBE FROM A DISTANCE OF 15 FEET.

	PERSON	UNDERHAND	OVERHAND
	1.	6	6
	2.	5	2
	3.	8	4
	4.	2	3
	5.	6	7
	6.	7	6
	7.	4	2
	8.	9	4
	9.	5	5
	10.	6	4
AVERAGE		5.8	4.3

In a test like this, someone had to organize the test and get 10 people to throw a ball 20 times in an attempt to get it through an innertube. Then they had to record the results comparing underhand and overhand throws and prepare averages for both. The results of these tests prove that accuracy was better throwing underhanded. In your tests, you will have to think of a similar method to document your results.

A PLAN

In your first meeting as a team, you must begin thinking of ways to teach people how to tie ties. The final method you select must provide the untrained a quick method for correctly making the appropriate knot in a tie while it is wrapped around his/her neck. Try to develop original but effective methods.

Your plan should include a variety of ideas considered and tested. Once you have agreed on the method, develop whatever materials will be required. When this is completed, test your program on a minimum of 10 people. Time them and record the results. Take another 10 people and time each of them giving each only a tie and the following set of verbal instructions:

1. Place the tie around your neck so that the wider portion is on your right side and extends closer to your waist by approximately 12 inches.

2. Hold one section with each hand and place the longer section on your right side over the other so that the two sections are now perpendicular to each other.
3. (You complete the instructions.)

Prepare the kind of forms that will be needed to record your tests. Consider a wide variety of ways to assist someone in easily tying a tie. You can use pictures, better instructions, video-tape, slides, models, or whatever you can "dream up."

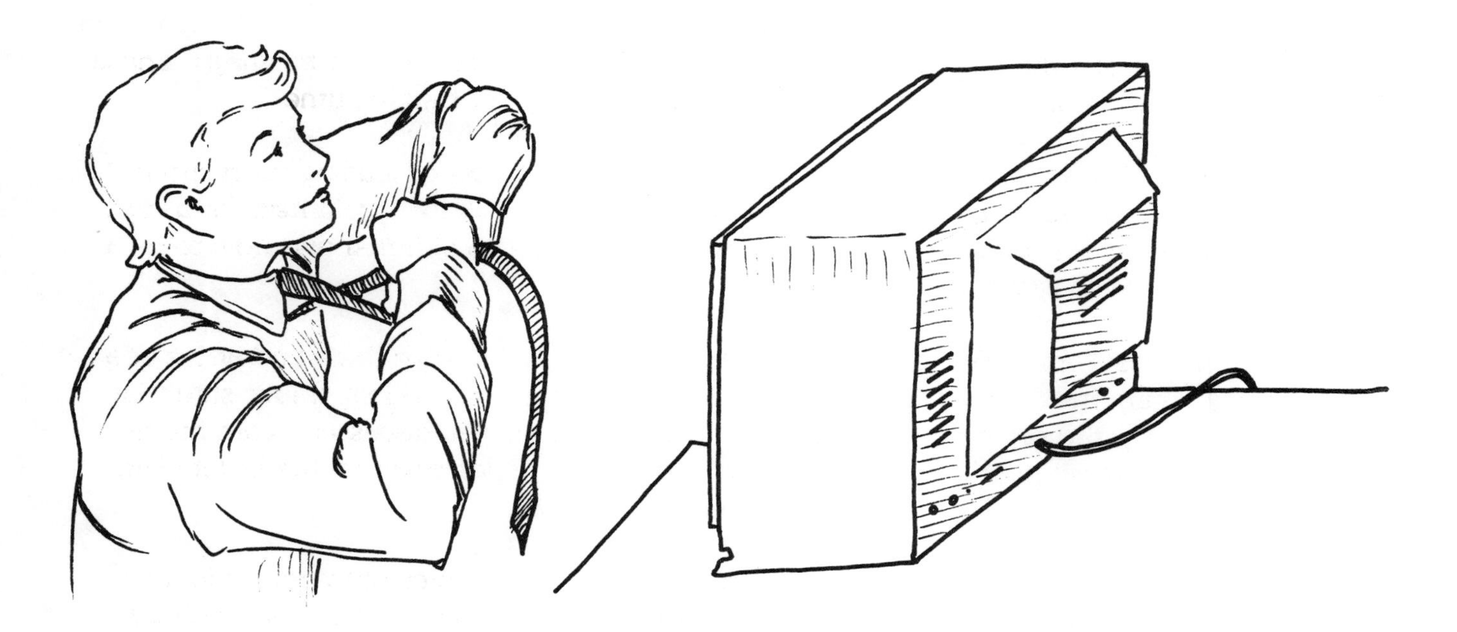

CLEAR ROLES

Select a chairperson from your team. It will be this person's job to assign the other responsibilities of team members (roles), call meetings, and make sure the project is completed on time.

Assignments must be explicit and deadlines established.

GROUND RULES

On projects like this it should be clear that people must attend meetings, that everyone will play different roles at different times, and that cooperation is important. Once a plan is in place, it should not be changed unless you can still meet the deadline. No matter how simple or difficult the project, do it as well as you can. Giving up or tuning out is a habit that gets harder to break the more it is done.

At your first team meeting, plan the next several meetings. The following are general agendas. Change them to suit your needs.

MEETING AGENDAS

#1 Select a chairperson. It will be his/her responsibility to get the job done by calling the meetings, guiding them, and assigning responsibilities.

Make sure that everyone is clear on what the project is and what has to be done.

Begin discussing ways of teaching people to tie ties. Try to develop novel ideas.

Assign everyone the responsibility of developing five ideas for the next meetings. These should be ideas on how to get someone to easily tie a tie for the first time.

Since it will be necessary to test your plan against the process of reading instructions "out loud," someone must finish writing the instructions. Ask for a volunteer (or assign someone) to complete the instructions. Select someone who either knows how to tie a tie or who could easily learn.

#2 Review ideas from each team member. As a group try to improve them and arrive at a choice. Team members should record the suggestions on their ballots. (Make sure that everyone has the same order.) Once all of the ideas have been discussed, team members should select their choice using the voting technique described on the ballot. The chairperson can tally the results and announce the winner.

Tallying the results is a matter of transferring team member votes onto one ballot and totalling them. The idea with the most points is the team choice. If there is a tie, you can either vote again or test both choices until it is clear that one works better than the other.

To get the project done within the 30 days, make a schedule of future meetings and what team assignments will be for those meetings. (Complete the "30-Day Planner.")

Review the written instructions assigned at the last meeting. Make sure that they are clear and ready to be used in tests. Assign someone the project of testing 10 people in tying ties using these written instructions. They must have the means to time each person being tested. Make up a form that can be used to tally the results of these tests. Assign a deadline to complete this task.

Assign team members the task of developing a procedure for using your improved idea for teaching someone to tie a tie. For example, if you decided that a series of drawings would be used, get them drawn. If you were going to show a video tape, make the video tape.

#3 Check the results of the testing. Hopefully, 10 tests have been conducted.

Review the progress in completing your new teaching method (i.e., the drawings or tapes). Decide how you will test 10 new people using your improved method. Select the people and the time of the tests.

#4 Take the test results from both series (i.e., the original ones using written instructions and the tests of your system) and decide how to present them in a group report to your class. Select someone to give the report. Arrange to make a poster or copies of your test data for distribution to the class. Plan a time to rehearse your presentation. Be ready when your teacher assigns the presentations.

Note that these have been recommendations only to illustrate the process of strategic thinking as a way of planning a project. You anticipate the steps in the overall project and you plan for them.

Feel free to organize the project in your own way.

Name ______________________________

BALLOT

POINTS	IDEA	DESCRIBE
______	1.	______________________________
______	2.	______________________________
______	3.	______________________________
______	4.	______________________________
______	5.	______________________________
______	6.	______________________________
______	7.	______________________________
______	8.	______________________________
______	9.	______________________________
______	10.	______________________________
______	11.	______________________________
______	12.	______________________________
______	13.	______________________________
______	14.	______________________________
______	15.	______________________________
______	16.	______________________________
5 total		

You have five points to distribute over your choices. You may allocate a maximum of three points to one choice. The total points allocated should equal five.

For example, you could select only two choices by allocating three points to your first choice and two points to your second choice. You could allocate two points to your first choice and one point for three others that you like.

Name____________________________

30-DAY PLANNER

Monday	Tuesday	Wednesday	Thursday	Friday